Secrets and Shortcuts

For Successful Writing

▼ ▼ ▼

You Can Learn from *My* Mistakes

R OCK VILLAG E
PUBLISHING

Middleborough, Massachusetts
First Printing

Secrets and Shortcuts
For Successful Writing
You *Can Learn from* My *Mistakes*
Copyright © 2009 by Edward Lodi

Typography and cover design by Carolyn Gilmore

ISBN 978-1-934400-14-2

Rock Village Publishing
41 Walnut Street
Middleborough MA 02346

(508) 946-4738

rockvillage@verizon.net

Contents

▼ ▼ ▼ ▼ ▼ ▼ ▼ ▼ ▼ ▼ ▼ ▼ ▼ ▼ ▼ ▼

Secrets and Shortcuts

For Successful Writing

▼ ▼ ▼

You Can Learn from *My* Mistakes

Preface

The idea for this book came about as a result of a talk I was asked to give on *Marmalade and Murder*, a mystery novel set on the cranberry bogs of southeastern Massachusetts. Actually, I've been asked to give the talk a number of times; it seems that libraries are eager to invite writers who are willing, not only to read from their books, but also to share the "secrets" of composition with the audience.

When I began putting together notes for the talk I quickly realized that I had more information to share than could possibly be squeezed into a brief afternoon or evening program. Even with outlines and handouts, and a question-and-answer session, the talk would scarcely touch upon the many facets of writing a mystery novel, or for that matter any other type of fiction.

The true secret to writing anything, of course, is hard work. If you are seriously interested in becoming a successful author, I cannot help you avoid the hours, days, weeks, years even, of toil needed to produce a worthwhile novel, short story, essay, play, or poem. But I can provide you with insights and most of the information you'll need to get started, and I can suggest shortcuts; *you* can learn from *my* mistakes.

And here's another secret: regardless of where your interests lie—whether in producing mystery novels, science fiction stories, humorous verse, memoirs, cookbooks, how-to-books, bodice-ripping romances, or the Great American Novel—you can learn from studying, and possibly trying your hand at, other genres. To give an extreme example, I have no intention of ever writing an epic poem, but I have learned a great deal about literature and the art of composition from studying masterpieces such as *Paradise Lost*. I shall probably never attempt to write a full-length play, but I have gained invaluable insights into the creative process from courses on Shakespeare and other dramatists taken in college and graduate school.

This is an exhortation, you see, to read every single chapter in this book. (And in the order in which they occur. Please don't skip around; conscientious writers, and editors, take great care in arranging the sequence of material in their books. They do so for a purpose.) Do not limit yourself to only those topics which you think will interest you most. For instance, the series of chapters beginning with "The Sweet and Sour of Writing Mystery Novels" defines and examines closely, and gives examples of, elements that are absolute requisites for any and all types of fiction: plotting, point of view, pacing, characterization, to name but a few. You won't be wasting your time learning about these things, even if your ambition is to write historical novels about piracy on the high seas, or fantasy novels about elves and trolls on Middle Earth. Every novel or short story requires characters, plot, pacing, and point of view—as well as any number of other "secrets."

The principle holds true for nonfiction—for essays, memoirs, histories, or biographies (again, to list just a few of the many categories). Even if your interest lies chiefly with one of these, you'll still want to learn all you can about the techniques used by successful fiction writers. Though relatively new, the term *creative nonfiction* describes a form of writing that has been around for centuries. "Creative" in this sense, of course, does not mean making things up—that would be a bit too creative! It does mean using all the language skills at your disposal to produce works of expository prose that command the same high levels of interest and excitement found in the best novels and short stories.

Dull indeed would be the biography that did not make at least occasional use of dialogue. An essay without a hook would be—well, most likely unread. Any piece of writing without pacing would be bumpy at best. Likewise, prose writers of any stripe can learn a heck of a lot from poets—a sense of the sounds of words, for example, as opposed to mere meaning; not to mention economy of language, and that oldest of rhetorical flourishes, rhythm.

What to write, ways to write, when to write, how to write—have I forgotten anything? Ah yes, *why* to write. In the pages that follow you'll find a discussion of these topics, and more, much more. You'll find the secret to eternal youth. (Not really; I just want to see if you're paying attention—though writing will help keep you young. Honest it will!)

Most of all, you'll discover—if you don't already know—the joy of working with words.

The juice of this book is concentrated, you see. Into this slender volume I've squeezed the essence of a lifetime—a lifetime devoted, to a large extent, to words: to reading; to studying and learning about language; and yes, to writing. Into it, along with more practical advice, I've tried to distill all the hard-won wisdom gained from decades of pushing pencils and pens and pounding away at the keys.

I've put this book together for your well-being and pleasure; so that taking advantage of my experiences—my many failures as well as my handful of successes—you can get a head start on your own writing, whether your goal is to write one book, or a hundred.

Edward Lodi
Rock Village
July 2008

A Life in the Day of a Writer

Is something amiss here? A *Life* in the *Day* of a Writer? There's a problem, surely, with this chapter heading. Is it time, perhaps, for an eye exam? Or to hire a competent proof reader?

No, dear reader, your eyes are not playing tricks on you. Nor does the title of this chapter contain an embarrassing typographical error. Although the focus will be on the daily routine of a writer—this writer in particular, but all other writers as well—the heading is an intentional play on words. To whit: when a writer sits down to the daily task of working with words, he or she brings a lifetime of experience to bear. Carrying the wordplay further, it is no exaggeration to say that to be truly successful, writers must—each and every day—bring *life* to their work.

Of course, they (as creator) have to breathe life into it, but that is an entirely different matter. That involves technique, acquired skills, tricks of the trade, knowledge gained by experience. These things—techniques, skills, tricks—will be dealt with in future chapters. Right now, though, the life I'm talking about is the life that is within you, the life that makes *you* a unique being. Call it spirit. Call it soul. Call it genius if you will, though you do not have to be a genius (in the modern sense) to be a successful writer, or even a great writer. (I'm using *genius* in its original sense, that of "guiding spirit.")

But first a caveat: we must not confuse soul, or spirit, in the sense we are talking here, with a related word, that chimera, that mythical being, that thing which has substance only in the fond minds of would-be writers (writers manqué), namely *inspiration*. Those who sit and wait for inspiration are waiting for Godot. Dismiss the false god of inspiration from your mind and replace it with that Holy Trinity: blood, sweat, and tears.

All of this (or none of this) will be made clear as you read along.

❖

"Where do you get your ideas?" That is a question which every writer is asked, time and time again. And of course the answer is, "How the hell do I know?"

No, the correct answer is, "The same place you get yours."

But that's no answer, is it? That's an evasion. That's making the person who asked the question feel a little foolish. Gee, maybe it's a dumb question. Or maybe he—Mr. Lodi—doesn't want to share his secrets. Maybe he's afraid I'll steal his ideas, or that my ideas will be better than his. Maybe he charges for ideas, and is reluctant to give away their source for free.

Once, when asked that question by an interviewer who was preparing an article for a local magazine, I replied: "There used to be an "800" number which I'd dial to obtain free ideas. But now I get them from the Internet. Would you like to know the website?" She nodded eagerly, and positioned herself to jot the information down on her legal pad.

I must confess I was embarrassed. I hadn't expected her to take me seriously.

So where do writers get their ideas?

From *life*!

Now, perhaps, you see what I mean by "A Life in the Day of a Writer."

So, the question really should be, "How do writers coax ideas into being?" That's a question I can answer, finally, without being a wise ass. (Speaking of asses, there's a donkey who lives down the street; in a moment I'll tell you how I've obtained ideas from him. You see, as a writer, you must be prepared to snatch, to borrow, to steal, your ideas from whatever source, including jackasses.)

The tried-and-true, time-honored (or any other tired, worn-out cliché that comes readily to mind) means of coaxing ideas into existence is to ask yourself, "What if…?" This, at least, is how ideas for stories and novels are born. What if a man fell asleep and woke up in another time, or dimension, or on another planet? What if animals could talk? What if a man (or woman) were marooned on a desert island? What if two people who hated one another were so marooned? What if your neighbor (the neighbor of *you*, the person reading these words)…what if your neighbor were a serial killer? What if he (or she) had a secret torture chamber in his cellar? What if while walking alone in the woods you fell down an abandoned well? What if…well, you get the idea.

Fuzzy is the name of the donkey who lives down the street. My wife and I, if we happen to be outdoors, sometimes hear him braying—which he does, at feeding time, VERY LOUDLY. I wrote a nature journal once, a day-by-day observation in poetry and prose of the changing seasons and of the animals and plants that throughout the year live on or visit our property on Walnut Street in Middleborough, Massachusetts. I called the book *Forty-One Walnut Street: A Journal of the Seasons* and dedicated it to "Fuzzy, the other jackass who lives on Walnut Street." We even held a ceremony in which we invited the press for a photo opportunity and presented Fuzzy with his own copy of the book. His picture made the front page of the local newspaper.

Where do writers get their ideas? I don't know, but having a donkey for a neighbor does open up possibilities.

A few years ago Fuzzy—who leads a pampered life—got loose from his barn. Not for the first time nor, I dare say, for the last; he's a donkey with wanderlust. He knows that there's a whole universe out there waiting to be explored—a fact of which you, as a writer, had better remind yourself, time and time again. You want ideas? Look around you! Anyhow, Fuzzy got loose and wandered down to the street about the same time, wouldn't you know, that the school bus came around the corner to pick up the neighborhood kids. Not being one to pass up an opportunity, Fuzzy got right in line with the students and entered the bus, or at least attempted to enter it; he got stuck in the doorway. (He's not one of those diminutive burros or puny little donkeys; in fact he's rather large for a jackass.) It took some doing, I'm told (alas, I wasn't there), to persuade Fuzzy to back down from the steps and onto the pavement again.

What if…

What if you were looking for ideas for a children's book, and you asked yourself, *What if a donkey got onto a bus and rode all the way to school?* What if he got off the bus and trotted into the school, and sat down at a desk? What if the children persuaded the teacher to let the donkey sit in on the class? The possibilities are endless. Although they are in actuality intelligent creatures (Fuzzy frequently outwits the person who "locks" him in the barn for the night), donkeys have an undeserved reputation for stupidity, which is really due to stubbornness; they do what *they* want to do, not what you want them to do; so in frustration you think they're stupid, when it's really you who are making an ass of yourself. That's why we refer to someone who does something stupid as a jackass. That's where the word *asinine* comes from.

What if the teacher treated the donkey as if he were a dunce, and compelled him to sit in a corner wearing a dunce cap? Or, what if Fuzzy got onto the bus and drove off in it? What if…ah, heck, *you* finish the damn story.

You want ideas? Look around you. Pay attention. To life. To language. To the jackass who lives up the street.

❖

Did someone say language? You want to be a successful writer? Then you darn well better pay attention to language. Better yet, you'd better have a love affair with it. That's what I did. I fell head over heels in love with language at an early age (long before I went to school) and have spent the rest of my life (so far!) pursuing it, caressing it, studying it, learning all I could about it: the words, the syntax, the history of its development. We're talking *English* here, of course, though the principle applies no matter what language you choose, or rather, which language chooses you. (I can think of only a handful of writers who achieved fame by writing in a language other than their native one: Joseph Conrad and Valdimir Nabakov come to mind, and perhaps a half dozen others.)

You don't have to be insanely in love with language to write a book, or any number of books. You may be in love with a discipline, such as history, or art, or one of the sciences, and write brilliant books on the subject. You may have a unique story to tell, or a cause to celebrate, or a special insight to share with the world. In these instances knowledge, or passion for your subject, will carry you through.

But if you want to be a Writer—someone who works with language, who shapes it, who creates with it, who knocks readers out of their socks (or lulls them into serene reveries)— then you must be enamored of words. You must find them sensuous, even sensual (and you must pay attention to, and have a high regard for, subtle differences—such as between *sensuous* and *sensual* !); you must long to touch, feel, smell, taste them, embrace them as you would a lover.

You must…well, you get the point.

Enough playing around with words (for the moment, anyhow). Let's look at a day in the life—as opposed to a life in the day—of a writer: a typical day in the life of someone who writes for a living.

Oops, there I go again. Leading the reader on, as it were. For the truth is, *there is no such thing*. As a typical day, that is. Or, yes, there may be such a thing, but it is so personal, so individual, so idiosyncratic, as to be atypical. What is typical for me will not necessarily (or even likely) be typical for you.

Some writers write every day. Others write only now and then. Some write five days a week, then take the weekend off. Others write only on weekends. Some write early in the morning, or all day long, or only at night, long after everyone else has gone to bed. Some write on the run, snatching ten or fifteen minutes here and there from an impossibly busy schedule. Some write on the bus, or the train, or while otherwise traveling. Some require solitude and absolute quiet. Others require solitude but with a background of music. Some choose to write in cafes, or libraries, or busy diners. Others write in their living room surrounded by spouse and children and anyone else who happens to drop by. Some write in bed.

Some finish a project—perhaps a book on which they've been working for years—then take a long sabbatical. Others (Trollop comes to mind) finish a novel, turn the manuscript page over, and immediately begin another. Some assign themselves a specific task: to write a certain number of words each day. It may be five hundred, it may be five thousand. Some may estimate the number of words they have written. Others will count each and every one, and once the goal has been reached, will stop writing for that day, even in the middle of sentence.

How often should *you* write? I recommend that you write every day. That, no matter how busy you think you are, you find a comfortable spot (or the only spot available to you) and write. Once you've been doing this—writing every day—for a number of years, and feel comfortable with yourself as a writer, you can tell me to go and take a flying leap; you can set your own schedule, and be typical in your own atypical way.

Do As I Say...

Do as I say…Not as I did. That is to say—as promised in the subtitle—*you* can learn from *my* mistakes.

Now Mr. Lodi—may I call you "Ed"?—surely, Ed, any mistakes which you *may have made in your, uh, distinguished career have been minimal.* N'est-ce pas?

Au contraire, dear reader. True, I have made very few blunders—only two in fact (two that I'll admit to; there may have been one or two others, but nothing truly momentous)—but the two blunders which I'll confess to were big ones.

Both were sins of omission.

The first thing I failed to do was to write. Even though from the age of five I knew with certainty—in my gut, in my heart of hearts, in the depths of my soul—that I wanted, more than anything else in the world, to be a writer when I grew up, I put off writing. I put it off for so long that I was forty years old before I began to publish with any regularity, mostly in regional magazines and literary journals. Forty years old!

And all the while there had been this snotty-nosed but bright-eyed little five-year-old beating with his fists against the walls of my psyche, crying to be let out.

What happened?

Well, I could say that life intervened; I did this, that, and the other.

Excuses! Nothing but excuses. I should have spent more time writing. But I didn't.

A truism which you may have heard is, well, all too true: Most people want to *have written*, but most people don't want to actually sit down (or stand—some writers, albeit only a few, prefer to stand while working)—most people don't want to sit down and write—hour after hour, day after day, week after week. For that's what it takes to become a writer. You've heard it before, and you'll hear it again. **If you want to be a writer, you must write.** Every day, if possible. And even if not possible. No matter how busy your schedule, you can always squeeze in a minute or two, at the least, to write.

So don't make the same mistake I made. Don't put off writing. Write now, today, no matter what your age, whether you're in school, in college, married with five children, retired, or in a nursing home. Write!

My wife and I do not watch television. We do not own a working set, nor have we owned one for these many years. If you find yourself without time to write, give up television. Completely. Never mind the news. Never mind the educational shows on PBS. Get rid of the damned thing!

If you have a lawn, get rid of that, too. Lawns are bad for the environment; they are useless to wildlife, they cause pollution, and they consume your valuable time. Replace every square inch of lawn with flowers, and shrubs (preferably those that attract butterflies and birds), and vegetables; get your exercise tending plants that will help this ailing planet. Or convert your lawn into a native wildflower garden, which requires minimal care. You want exercise? Go for a walk each day; doing so will help clear your mind. Your writing will improve immensely. Trust me.

Stop wasting time on your cell phone. Get rid of it! (Okay, you can keep it for emergencies. But don't use it for idle chatter.) Limit your time on the Internet. Blah blah blah. You don't want to hear a sermon, nor do I wish to preach one, so I'll say no more about ways you can trade the moments which you may be wasting in exchange for more time to write. Just take the word of a reformed sinner: write!

But don't think that serious writing comes without cost. You may—you probably will have to—give up your social life. Or at least most of it. You can still retain a friend or two—those who'll stick by with you, who'll understand when, repeatedly, time after time, you politely decline their invitations because you cannot spare the time from your writing; and who won't feel too hurt when you fail to invite them, because you're far too busy writing to give a party, or have people over for dinner, or for a glass of wine or a cup of tea.

Yeah, perhaps I'm exaggerating a tad. You *can* be a writer, and still have a social life. But it won't be easy.

Sports? Forget about sports. You won't have time for them. Unless, of course, you become a sports writer, in which case you can eat your cake and have it, too.

The second sin of omission, related to the first, is a failure to keep a journal, or a diary, or a notebook. Not having done so is by far the single greatest regret of my life.

Why keep a journal? What are the benefits?

Discipline, for one. The discipline of writing regularly, preferably every day, or even several times a day. If you get into the habit of writing regularly early enough in life—as a young child—you are guaranteed to become a writer. You may choose not to pursue writing as a career, or even as an avocation, but you will possess the skills and the temperament of an accomplished writer, should you need to call upon them.

Another benefit: developing your powers of observation. If you keep a journal, and write in it faithfully, you will need things to put into it. Things that you see, hear, feel. (Or better yet, imagine. But that's another matter.) Jotting down impressions of people whom you meet, or objects that you encounter, or the natural world that surrounds you, or what you will—will develop your descriptive skills, not to mention your mastery over language. It will make you into a person who thinks, who reflects, who ponders. It could make you into a poet! Or a scientist—one who not only observes with a keen eye, but who also is able to communicate to others his or her insights and discoveries.

And keeping a journal will give you a wealth of material to draw upon in later life—material for writing memoirs, or history, or novels and short stories. I spent the most exciting three years of my life, in my twenties, after graduate school, in the Civil Rights Movement. And I failed to keep a journal! I met any number of famous people—people who were famous then, or who achieved fame afterwards. And I failed to keep a journal!

That failure is, I am convinced, the reason why, even though I have so far written more than twenty books, I have neglected to write about that most important period of my life. I have tried to write about it, both fiction and nonfiction, but my attempts have all ended in frustration. I cannot remember the details—the little things, the nuances, that make history (or fiction) come alive.

I lived history, was a part of it. And flubbed it as a writer.

But—and here I go again—it's never too late to begin to keep a journal, such as the nature journal I kept, the day to day observations and reflections which eventually became the book dedicated to my donkey pal, Fuzzy.

But you don't have to write about nature (though you really should, if only to hone your skills); you can record your impressions of the books you read, or the movies you see, or the music you listen to—that's how critics are made! You can describe the people you meet, and imagine their inner lives—that's how novelists and short-story writers are born.

So the lesson of this chapter is, learn from my mistakes.
Write write write. And keep a journal. Or a notebook. Or a diary.
But there's another lesson, too. (More important, perhaps, than the other two.) And that lesson is, it's never too late. No matter what your age, or circumstances, begin to write now. Keep that journal. Do as I say. But if you begin late, then do as I did.

Let's Get Physical

The second most frequently asked question of writers (after "Where do you get your ideas?") is, "How do you write—with a computer?" or some variation, such as "Do you write longhand?" Though the physical method of composition may, at first thought, seem unimportant, the question is by no means frivolous. Many writers—including some of the greatest and / or most successful—are very particular as to how they convey words onto paper (or into electronic format).

A few, believe it or not, still compose in longhand, using pencil or pen. These authors may go through a daily ritual of sharpening a certain number of pencils, which they line up in neat rows. Of if their weapon of choice is the pen, they may be extremely fussy as to the color of the ink; for some black is *de rigueur;* for others (poets no doubt), only

> a certain hue
> of blue
> will do.

The paper they select is important, too. Some prefer yellow legal pads; others cheap composition books; others nothing but sheets of the finest custom-made paper. Such writers maintain that the sensation of physically shaping words is vital to their creativity.

Most writers nowadays use computers or some other form of word processing, but by no means all. Some (one of whom I know personally) prefer to bang away at the keys of old-fashioned manual typewriters; others are quite content with (also old-fashioned) electric, or electronic, typewriters. There are even some who dictate, either to a machine, or to a flesh-and-blood human being.

What about you, Ed? (You did say I could call you "Ed"?) How do you compose?

I, dear reader, use a computer—a rather old one, to which I have grown inordinately attached. The software, though antiquated, suits me just fine. (I'm told that the day rapidly approaches when floppy discs will become obsolete. Oh, what shall I do then?)

I began, however, by writing longhand, with pencil. And did so for many years, until the pain and stiffness of arthritis made it impracticable. In those halcyon days of heedless youth I would write the final draft (after numerous pencil revisions) on a manual typewriter, though towards the end I went modern and switched to electric.

If asked for advice (and even if not asked!), I would suggest that you write using whatever device works for you. You might even want to try your hand (long or otherwise) at more than one method. Flexibility is the key word here. Eschewing the modern world, you may, on occasion, want to sit quietly with sharpened pencil and ready pad by a purling brook, and let your thoughts flow in harmony with the limpid waters.

You may even, if only just the once—and who knows, it might become a habit—enjoy the sensation of bending over an antique typewriter as you clack away imagining yourself Hemingway in the throes of inspired composition. Or (as I did once) you may want to sit at a desk with a quill pen clenched tight in your fist, ink blotter close by, and pretend to be Jane

Austen. With luck, as your fingers relax and the tip of the feather tickles your nose, words will as if by magic sprout in fanciful script on the face of the pristine paper. But beware! The spirits of Austen or Hemingway may be hovering about; they may choose to haunt you; they may enter your dreams, or even your soul, and then you'll find yourself in a fine fix: a writer for life!

Keep in mind, of course, that no matter which method you choose by which to create literary masterpieces, the final version of your deathless creation will have to be submitted (to an agent, publisher, or printer) in electronic form.

Acquiring Skills

So, Mr. Lodi—sorry, but somehow I don't feel comfortable addressing you by your nickname. "Ed" seems too familiar; there's something strange about you, Mr. Lodi, something off-putting "What ho! what ho! this fellow is dancing mad! / He hath been bitten by the Tarantula."

*So—Mr. Lodi—you've gone to great lengths to tell me more than I ever cared to know about goose quill pens, pads of yellow or white paper, not to mention outmoded typewriters, or for that matter the gibbering ghosts of Jane Austen or Ernest Hemingway. But— other than reading widely, or attending special classes—how in blue blazes do I learn how to **WRITE**?*

If you ask me, you've wasted precious time and paper (whether white, yellow, or sky-blue pink!) beating about the bush, as it were.—[signed] Your Dubious Reader

Humph—there's no pleasing some people. Perhaps I'm mistaken, but didn't I mention, once or twice (a little irony here), that the secret to learning how to write is by **writing**? ARE YOU DEAF? I'll repeat myself: it's simple; you sit down, and you write, and you write, and you write. At some point—fifteen or twenty years later, let us say—you rise from your chair, and lo and behold, you are now a full-fledged writer.

Though—to be fair to our Dubious Reader—beyond sheer perseverance there are one or two requisites to becoming an accomplished writer. Mastery of language comes to mind. This may sound obvious, but I have encountered any number of *soi-disant* "authors" whose attitude seems to be that innate brilliance, or mere sensationalism, or novelty of ideas, or intensity of passion, are sufficient in and of themselves to produce a readable book. Let someone else—an agent or an editor, say, or some other lowly peon—worry about the niceties of grammar and syntax.

Such an attitude may work if you're a celebrity, especially one of notoriety, with an explosive story to tell (i.e., sell). If that's the case—if your name is a household word (better yet, a name that's whispered or not spoken at all in front of the children)—then editors will fall all over themselves in their mad scramble to be the lucky one chosen to publish your "book," even if they have to hire a ghostwriter to do the actual writing.

It may likewise work very well if you're a famous athlete or movie star—or married to one.

But if, like me, you're a relative nobody, just an average "Joe" or "Jane" (or "Ed"—and just what, O Dubious One, do you mean by "dancing mad"?), then you'd best learn the basics of standard English. Whether you're a student still in school, at whatever level, or an adult with access to Continuing Education, take all the English courses offered. Study Grammar. Composition. Literature. Creative Writing. Though be warned: Creative Writing classes can be risky; a poor teacher or vindictive classmates can stifle creativity. I've never taken a course in Creative Writing, and believe that I am the better for not having done so, but there are those who swear by them—who go so far as to insist on the necessity of obtaining a Master's Degree in the subject. But then, what need have you, Dear Reader, for

Creative Writing courses?—you're reading this book. How better to learn the craft of writing?

Ahem! [sound of throat being cleared, in the exaggerated manner of one desirous of expressing skepticism or disdain.]

Oh, so it's you again, Dubious Reader. How rude to interrupt. This is what I get, I suppose, for being just a regular guy, for allowing you to become over familiar; it just proves the old adage, that no good deed goes unpunished. Dancing mad, am I? Bitten by the tarantula? I'll give *you* tarantulas, aplenty!

[sounds of mirthless laughter, and of a door being slammed.]

Poor sport, that fellow. Can't take a joke. Good riddance, I say.

Moving forward…

If by some great good fortune you have the opportunity to study Latin, by all means do so. Even a rudimentary knowledge of this so-called dead language will increase your word power immeasurably; more than half our English words derive, directly or indirectly, from Latin. Moreover, the study of Latin grammar (and this is true for all foreign languages) will provide you with invaluable insights into the structure of English.

A useful exercise—one I never resorted to, but which some writers say has helped them in the early stages of their development—is to choose a passage from an admired writer and copy it out, in longhand. Doing this often enough, it is alleged, will imprint a sense, however vague, of the favored author's style, and will help the budding writer to the development of a style of his or her own. (Perhaps I should have included this tip in the "Let's Get Physical" chapter; the trick may lie in the nerve patterns, or connections, that are established by the simple act of the hand tracing words on paper.) Who knows? Such an exercise may be worth a try.

Though I wonder—in this age of mindless technology, is the art of handwriting—penmanship—still taught? Or has it gone the way of the barbershop quartet?

A trick which in my feckless youth I did resort to, many times (more than a hundred), was to take troubling aspects of usage, grammar, or diction, and write about them, in clever (well, I thought they were clever) and humorous vignettes. At first I chose as subjects for these little sketches matters that troubled me—parts of speech, let us say, that I found myself repeatedly looking up in the dictionary: for example, the past participles for the verbs *to lie* and *to lay*. Rather than try to memorize these little devils, why not, by making them the subject of a miniature essay, fix them in my mind once and for all?

So that's what I did; I fiddled around with them (my favorite pastime is, after all, playing with words) and when I was satisfied with the result, sent it off to the editor of an obscure newsletter for aspiring authors. She—the poor dear must have been desperate for fillers that issue—accepted it; that acceptance prompted me to write other little monographs and send them off, to her, and to other editors as well. In the course of a few years I sold dozens of these things. Admittedly, "payment" often came in the form of contributor's copies, or subscriptions to the journal or magazine. But once in a while it came in the form of a check. Imagine—being paid to play with words!

If you're curious to read that first vignette, the one on *lie* and *lay*, I've included it, along with others, in an appendix at the end of this book. If you take the time to read the appendix you will, in all probability, pick up a few pointers on language; and who knows—you may be inspired to write little essays of your own, and send them off, whether to print journals, or over the Internet.

Writer's Block

There are those who will tell you, with a curl of their lip and a supercilious smile, that there is no such thing as writer's block, that it is all a figment of your imagination. These are the same folks, no doubt, who maintain that addiction, or depression, or insomnia, are all in the mind; that all it takes to overcome these supposed maladies is a little bit of will power, or common sense, or bracing up.

You just stubbed your toe? Funny, *I* don't feel a thing.

The love of your life died a week ago? Tough luck; a real shame. But isn't it time to stop grieving and get on with your life?

Someone else's pain is easy to bear, easy to dismiss, easy to deride. Or so it would seem, with those who maintain (usually with a superior air) that writer's block does not exist.

What, by the way, is writer's block?

Writer's block, dear friend, is the inability to write. Not from lack of skills, of course—only writers (including previously prolific and / or successful writers) get writer's block. The condition occurs when words refuse to flow—or even to trickle. It may be caused by depression, or something equally insidious. You, the writer, sit down to blank paper, or a blank screen, and an hour later you are still staring at the blankness. Likewise, two hours later. The rest of the day. The next day. The next week. For some, the condition my last for years, or even forever, i.e., the remainder of their lifetime.

The words do not flow? Come now, you may be muttering, how often do the words actually flow? Don't most writers have to struggle, a word, a sentence, a paragraph at a time? Is not the flow more like a drip?

Yes. And no. Sometimes, when you're lucky, the words do flow. They pour out onto the page as if, somehow, you'd tapped the Mother Lode. The definition of *flow* will differ, of course, from writer to writer. For some, a half day's session resulting in five hundred words is cause for rejoicing; for others, nothing fewer than five thousand would be cause to bring out the champagne.

On the other hand, for some the words seldom, or never, flow. But they do—somehow—trickle. The trickle may not be steady, or even on a pace with cold molasses. But, over time, the words, however slowly, come; they accumulate.

The insidious thing about writer's block is that whatever words do make it to page or screen are totally worthless. They're insipid. They limp; they're lame. In the words of the Bard, they're stale and profitless.

A fairly common cause for writer's block (I'm told) is too-quick success. A young writer's first book becomes an instant best-seller, or is widely acclaimed; it receives a lot of attention, and earns its author tons of money, or at least a lucrative contract for additional books. Overwhelmed (with self-doubt perhaps, the feeling that the first book was only a fluke, that it would be impossible to write a second equally good, let alone better), the young author suddenly finds him- or herself unable to write—suffers from writer's block, that is.

You or I should be so lucky! Most of us—those who at one time or another suffer from the agonies and frustrations of writer's block—do not come down with the malady because of too-easy or early success. We come down with it from mundane—often unknown—causes.

I know. I suffered from writer's block for twenty years.

I'm not exaggerating. As a school kid, especially in high school, I was a whiz at writing. I loved words. I loved reading, and studying, and writing. I looked forward to writing compositions for English class. My efforts were often singled out for praise, even passed around from teacher to teacher. Out of a class of one hundred and fifty, I was valedictorian—mostly because of my facility with words.

Then came college, and with it, writer's block.

That is not to say that I could not write at all. *Au contraire.* In college, and then in graduate school, I wrote any number of term papers. Admittedly, they tended to be somewhat stiff, or stilted—though aren't academic papers supposed to be, if not pedantic, then at least formal?—but they did the trick. They usually received an A, or at the least, a B+. I could write term papers—but nothing else. Nothing creative.

I knew, in the depths of my soul, that I was a writer. And yet, try as I might, I could not write. It was only in my late thirties that I began to break through the block so that, one at a time, the words began to trickle, and eventually, to flow.

What went wrong?

More to the point, what can *you* learn from *my* mistakes?

Self-analysis is probably not my greatest strength, but I would nonetheless hazard the guess that, knowing that I had no greater desire in life other than to be a writer—not necessarily a great author, or a best-selling one, but someone who spent his days writing, and making, however modest, a living at it—I felt (at a sub-conscious level) overwhelmed by the immensity of the work ahead of me. Or, more likely, majoring in English Literature, and reading the very greatest writers of all ages (including those who wrote in languages other than English), I felt intimidated, utterly unequal to the task.

I made the mistake—which you can, which you must, avoid—of comparing my own humble efforts to the greatest works ever written. Believe me, doing so is a fool's exercise.

Smart writers—which I certainly wasn't at the time—are content to begin modestly—to write the best that they can at the time, without striving to write (absurd as it sounds) on the level of Shakespeare or Jane Austen. Oh, by all means give yourself the goal of writing—someday—the Great American Novel, or the world's best epic poem, or the greatest "whatever"—but plan to do so gradually, in steps. It's okay, in other words, to begin by writing merely a Good American Novel, or a fine lyric poem. If you can convince yourself that what you are writing has merit—and that, no matter what level you are currently at, your writing will improve over time—then you will have a good chance of avoiding the murderous pitfall known as Writer's Block.

Now that we've got the pep talk over with, let's get on to the real substance of this chapter: how to get through writer's block if, despite all your self-knowledge, you find yourself afflicted with it.

The first thing you do, is admit to yourself that you have it. An alcoholic who denies having a drinking problem is unlikely to find a cure. This may sound obvious—so much good advice in life does, once you've heard it—but there are those who tell themselves that their failure to write is due merely to the fact that inspiration has not yet struck. They'll begin to write, as soon as they feel inspired.

The trouble is, they never feel inspired—whatever "inspired" means. Does it mean that the Muse of Poetry suddenly feels disposed to whisper sweet nothings into your ear, so that you begin to dash off faultless lyrics in rhymed iambic pentameter, one after the other? Or does it mean that, out of the blue, you will be possessed by an idea—that the entire plot and cast of characters of a novel on the scope of *War and Peace* will reveal themselves to you in a dream, or while you're taking a shower?

Short of a miracle—and you know how rare miracles are—inspiration will only strike those who write. And write. And write. Who, in other words, have written—a great deal.

Okay, so you confess to yourself that yeah, maybe you've got a touch of that disease, or disorder, or what have you, known as Writer's Block. Now what?

Look for the root cause of it. You may never discover the cause—and a cure does not absolutely depend on finding it—but having an idea as to the possible cause or causes for your particular case of writer's block is the first step in getting rid of the damned thing. Is it because you're too hard on yourself? That as soon as you put a few words down, on paper or screen, your internal editor—that little all-knowing voice inside you—says, nah, that's not good enough. Do you feel, somehow, unworthy? Who would want to read what you have to say, anyhow?

The answer to that last question is, of course, any number of people. We're all human; we're all in this together. Your feelings are as genuine, as valid, as mine, or anyone else's. Your ideas are as potentially worthy. (I say potentially, only because they may require a little development.) As for that all-knowing internal editor, turn a deaf ear to it. Tell it—and yourself—that the words that you are currently putting down are only temporary, that you will be revising them shortly. Which, to be sure, is exactly what you will be doing. Remember: writing is re-writing. Writing is revising—over and over again.

Once you sincerely believe that you have as much right to write—to call yourself a writer—as the next guy, you will have gone a long way in dispelling any symptoms of writer's block that may have been plaguing you. You will write, you will revise, and at some point you will submit your work for publication. Chances are, that work will be rejected—time and time again. That fact, however, will not deter you (will not bring on writer's block). You will continue to write, and to submit, and as I will say, and reiterate, time and time again in this book, *you will at some point succeed.*

Still feeling blocked? It's worse than constipation, isn't it?

Despair not. The cure is just around the corner. (Well, maybe around a few corners. Quite a few corners. But it is there, believe me.) What you do is, you force yourself to write. *I* did, when I was blocked. (Trouble is, I didn't do it often enough. That's why it took me twenty years to cure my own case.) Sit down and write. If nothing happens, give yourself an assignment. It may be to write an entry in your journal. Describe the weather. Or write about the meals you've eaten—or expect to eat—that day. Describe them. Discuss, on paper or screen, their nutritional value. Or write about someone you know; or about your feelings regarding an important political issue. Do this for as long as time allows. Two or three hours, at the least. Do this every day. Time and time again. It's boring, it's frustrating, but it works.

I wrote three (execrable) novels while suffering from writer's block. That's the commendable part. The less than commendable part is that it took me twenty years to write them.

Had I known what I know now—had someone given to me the advice I'm giving to you—I probably could have written through the block in twenty weeks, or even twenty days. Alas, as the saying goes, "We get too late too smart."

The Sweet and Sour of Writing a Mystery Novel

It took me two and one-half years to write my first mystery novel, *Marmalade and Murder*. Or rather, it took me four and one-half decades. Or somewhere in between; it all depends on when you start the clock ticking. Is it the day when I grabbed a yellow legal pad and jotted down a half dozen ideas for plot, setting, characters? Or the day when the notion first entered my mind that a particular setting—in this case a cranberry bog—might make the ideal backdrop for murder and mayhem? Or the day—nearly a half century ago—when I knew for sure that I would sit down and write a mystery—some day.

The first day of the two-and-one-half-year period is emblazoned in memory. My wife and I were in Bar Harbor, Maine, for a brief stay prior to attending a Down East birding festival on Campobello Island. Our timing, though, was bad; we were experiencing a nor'easter. Venturing out of our hotel room meant an instant soaking. But why would we venture out? The flooded roads were impassable; there was nowhere to go.

My wife and I do not watch television. At home we do not even own a set.

There was nothing for me to do, except write.

I had no excuse, finally, for not committing myself to the long, arduous task of writing a mystery novel—a task doubly arduous, in that mysteries require a lot more rote thinking than most other types of novels. You've got to write them twice, really. Twice, not in the sense of revision, because a good writer will do a dozen or more of those, but twice in the sense that you have to write it once backwards in your head, and then once again forward, on paper or on the keyboard. But I'll come to all that later.

As a lifelong fan of mystery and detective fiction I've read thousands of novels and short stories; for more than a decade, in the 1980's and '90's, I reviewed mysteries for *The Armchair Detective*—I pulled apart and analyzed from top to bottom scores of full-length novels and short story collections. Over the years I wrote enough short stories in the field to fill a slender volume of my own: *Murder on the Bogs* (now out of print). I've also written about twenty other books, some of them, like horror and ghost stories, close relatives to the mystery.

The important consideration is that having written my very own mystery novel, I am now in a position to help you get started on yours. Using *Marmalade and Murder* as a referent, I am prepared to share with you whatever knowledge and insight I've gained from years of experience as reviewer, editor, and teacher, and from firsthand experience.

I can't tell you how to write *your* mystery novel, but I can tell you how I wrote mine. I may even be able to give you some insights into the writing process, though I can't make any promises that what works for me will work for you.

My wife writes cookbooks. Not only do I get to taste-test her creations, but I also proofread the actual recipes. So I have some idea of how, let's say, a cake is made. I know that a cake requires certain ingredients, that these ingredients have to be prepared in a certain way, and added in a certain order, and mixed accordingly, and then baked at a precise temperature for a specified period of time.

Writing a mystery novel is a lot like baking a cake. There's a recipe that you have to follow. But I must warn you: whereas the cake recipe calls for exact measurements—a cup of this, a tablespoon of that, one and one-half cups of something else— the recipe for writing a mystery is a lot less precise. It calls for a pinch of this, a dash of that, a handful of something else. You bake it at whatever temperature, until done.

In other words, as with any recipe there are necessary ingredients, but there is no tried-and-true formula. You know, for example, that you need a plot, and a setting, and a certain number of suspects, and things called clues and red herrings. But when it comes down to what exactly constitutes a dash or a pinch of these things, or just how many dashes or pinches are required, you're pretty much on your own.

A logical place to begin our discussion would probably be with definitions of certain terms—those "ingredients" I've been talking about. **Plot, setting, point of view** come to mind. These, along with many others, are necessary ingredients to any mystery novel. But the most logical place is not always the best.

Definitions are, to a large extent, abstractions. What I'd like to do—and will do, if it's all the same to you—is begin with something a bit more concrete: just one "ingredient," which I'll define and give an example of and then—as it were—beat to death, or at least rake over the coals. (You'll have to bear with me; I can't resist using these clichés for their gruesome associations, so fitting for a discussion of books about murder and other heinous crimes.) Once we've fully examined this one ingredient, we'll be able to use it as the basis for describing others.

❖

Every mystery novel—every novel for that matter, regardless of genre; every short story; and most books in general—needs a hook.

The **hook** is the device by which you catch your fish—the reader. You will eventually have your bait: a bound copy of the book, along with the title, and perhaps an enticing cover design. The reader nibbles at the bait by picking up the book, examining the dust jacket, perusing the first page, and beginning to read. But he or she will continue to read only if properly hooked. Ideally, you should hook your reader with the first sentence. Certainly you must do so with the first two or three sentences. There are far too many good books in the world for readers to waste their time on those which do not interest them. You must snare their interest immediately. You do this, not by the beauty and brilliance of your prose, or the wisdom and profundity of your thoughts—this is after all a mystery novel—but by piquing their curiosity. Having read the first sentence or two, they must continue reading, to find out what happens next.

And you must hold that interest, word by word, sentence by sentence, chapter by chapter, for the entire two or three hundred pages of your novel.

For a number of reasons, which I'll explain as I go along, I began *Marmalade and Murder* with a **prologue**—an introductory section which, though essential to the story, is separated from the main body by some element, such as time, or space, or point of view. You do not, of course, need a prologue; most novels lack one. Think of it as an option, something you'll use only if it works for your particular book. But whether you choose to begin with a Prologue or with Chapter One, you must hook the reader immediately.

Let's take a close look at the opening paragraph of *Marmalade and Murder*:

> This was the first time, ever, that she had been by herself in the woods, the first time she had strayed so far from home. Pudges, although he was her best friend, did not count as a companion. How could he? He was only a dog, a mixed-breed with pointed muzzle and short fuzzy legs.

How successful are these four short sentences in hooking the reader?

The first sentence tells us that a female is alone in the woods. This fact in itself alerts us to the possibility of danger. We know that this is a mystery novel; we know that it has the word *murder* in the title. Females alone in the woods are vulnerable; they are sometimes murdered. Moreover, this first sentence implies that the female may be a child: not only is she alone in the woods for the first time, it is also the first time she has strayed so far from home. The next three sentences reinforce what the first sentence has told us: she is alone, with only her *little* dog (those "short fuzzy legs") for company. And she has *strayed*.

If the hook has succeeded—by causing concern for the young girl's safety—the reader will want to continue, if only for another sentence or two.

> She could hear the shouts of the others as they played on in the field without her. Filtered through the trees, the echoes of their laughter seemed loud yet remote, like the blare of a TV abandoned at full volume in a far-off room. Hearing the familiar voices calling to one another made her feel safe.

This short paragraph reinforces the sense of isolation. Her friends are playing "without her." The "echoes" are "remote;" the words "abandoned" and "far-off" occur. The final sentence has a chilling effect: hearing the voices of her friends makes *her* feel safe, but *we*, as adults, know better. Since this is a mystery novel, something bad may happen to this child. The reader continues, not necessarily with feelings of dread, but at least with mild apprehension.

> The gray squirrel—whose antics, while foraging on the ground, had enticed Pudges to go charging into the pine grove in hot pursuit—had long ago vaulted up the trunk of a tall tree and vanished. As it scampered high into the boughs she had caught a last glimpse of its bushy tail, like a hand waving goodbye. Now as she craned her neck to seek out the squirrel's hiding place, she saw how the interlocking branches of the trees, like hairy, monstrous arms groping outward, met from both sides of the trail in the middle, and clenching their fingers, blocked out the sun.

> Being on a path deep in the woods was like being at the bottom of a long, dimly lit tunnel.

This passage serves to heighten a sense of danger, even terror. The branches are "hairy, monstrous arms;" they're groping, clenching, blocking out the sun. The squirrel has "disappeared;" its vanishing tail is like a hand waving goodbye. There's an ominous finality to that word, "goodbye." And our child thinks of herself as being "at the bottom of a long, dimly lit tunnel." This creates a sense of claustrophobia; where does the tunnel lead?

> The squirrel's disappearance did not deter Pudges from dashing madly along the pathway. In typical dog fashion he paused now and again to snuffle with his nose against the ground, all the while yipping or glancing up at her expectantly. His brown fur, all the way up to his belly, was matted with mud.

Not a great deal going on here—except that the dog is leading her ever deeper into the woods, and its "yipping" (rather than barking) reminds us that it is a little dog and therefore not much protection against potential danger. Incidentally, the mention of mud is more than just visual description; it is also a **foreshadowing** of something that will happen later—though of course it will only be of significance with hindsight.

> Although this was a part of town into which she had never before ventured, she knew that she would not become lost, because she could always follow Pudges's muddy paw prints (as well as her own footprints!) back along the trail to the place where she had left her fellow adventurers. Even so, she wondered

whether she ought to turn back to rejoin the others. Some of them had bicycles; they might not wait for her before heading for home; they might forget about her entirely.

That sense of isolation... Her doubts about proceeding...And yes—that mention of mud again.

Although it was not anywhere near supper time, it was growing late. Already the sun had sunk low in the sky, and it was dark in the woods, just a little bit scary. But then again, she was nine years old, quite capable of taking care of herself.

And Pudges insisted on continuing their explorations; she would venture just a little bit farther along the wooded path, to see what lay ahead.

It's growing late, the sun is sinking, it's dark and scary in the woods. And now we know for sure what we've suspected all along: she's a very young child. Only nine years old. She may not know what lies ahead. But we do, or think we do.

Suddenly the forest ended and she found herself on a strip of cleared ground along the shore of what looked like a small lake, but which she knew was only a cranberry bog flooded for the winter. There was a similar bog not far from where she lived on which she had gone skating hundreds of times. This bog, though, was much larger than the one near her home.

There's nothing ominous here; in fact, we're relieved that she's out of the woods. But since we've read this far, we may as well continue on a bit. Besides, this being a mystery novel, we as experienced readers know that the little girl is, if you'll forgive the pun, not out of the woods yet.

> Across the bog, at the edge of a vast tract of swamp, she caught sight of something moving—something bulky. It was only a glimpse, really: of a vague shadow that shuffled along before turning to merge with the underbrush. She strained her eyes, but whatever it was that she had seen had disappeared—and was certainly nothing to be concerned about, with Pudges there to protect her. A bear perhaps? But that was nonsense. There were no bears in this part of Massachusetts. A hunter, maybe. Or even a deer. Wait till the others heard that she had seen a deer!

That sense of relief which the reader felt when the little girl left the woods—it was, as we suspected all along, only a tease! Up till now the typical reader has experienced only the vaguest sense of unease, only the vaguest foreboding of evil. But now we have something decidedly concrete to worry about. Just what is it, we wonder, that the little girl (*our* little girl, for by now we have a vested interest in her well-being)—just what is it that she has caught a glimpse of lurking near the swamp? Whatever it is, we know that it's vague, bulky, shuffling. And we are conscious of the fact that the little girl is in the midst of a sort of wilderness—surrounded by woods, a flooded cranberry bog, and a vast *swamp*.

And then there's that childish false sense of security she feels.

She assures herself that she has nothing to fear—"with Pudges there to protect her." But *we* know better, don't we?

Incidentally, now is a good time to mention something which may be obvious but which should never be taken for granted: that no matter how wrapped up you the author are in creating the story, in getting it all down on paper (or into the guts of a computer), in thinking up plot devices and moving characters along—your primary concern is always the reader.

You must constantly ask yourself: how will this—this word, this image, this phrase, this sentence—affect the reader? At every moment you must ask yourself what the reader is thinking, feeling. And you are obligated to do this without ever calling attention to yourself.

Your primary goal in *writing* is to make the reader forget that he or she is *reading*.

Let's return to the prologue:

Meanwhile, Pudges bounded onto the ice.

She had been repeatedly warned that, even though it was still winter and the weather felt cold, the ice might not be safe in all places and she was never to go out onto it without her parents' permission. She was especially not to go onto it when she was all by herself.

But this ice looked safe. It was thick and there were no cracks in it. It held Pudges just fine. True, he was neither a big dog, nor a heavy

dog. But he had four legs. If the ice was safe
for Pudges with his *four* legs—wasn't it comical the way he pranced about, as if the cold
tickled the bottoms of his paws!—it was surely
safe for her, who had only *two* legs. Besides,
she would step carefully and not go out very
far.

Here's a new twist. All along we've been thinking murder, or at least harm to the child from a human source. But now
we're confronted with an entirely unexpected danger: thin ice.
And if we, the reader, have been paying attention, we'll recall
the several references to mud: if the ground itself is not frozen,
the ice is surely not safe.

See! It held her just fine. It was slippery…but
that was because there was just the thinnest
sheet of water coating the surface.

Our fears for the little girl have been realized: she has
ventured onto the ice. And we know for certain that the ice is
definitely unsafe, with water coating the surface. It is the rare
reader who would stop reading at this point.

Out of the corner of her eye, in the place
where she had seen the bear, or deer, or whatever it might have been, she saw a figure
emerge from the swamp and begin to run
toward her. At about the same time that she
saw the man, for that is what it turned out to
be, she felt the ice buckle beneath her. Fright-
ened, she turned to retrace her steps, but despite her frantic efforts to reach shore the ice

gave way completely, and she plunged into
the water. She sank all the way to her knees
before her feet touched bottom.

Here, we have two things happening at once. Sure
enough, just as we feared, the child falls through the ice. But
there is hope: she sinks only to her knees; and a man is running
to help her.

Or is he? He's running toward her, of that we may be
certain—but is it to help? This is, after all, a murder mystery.
We can never be sure that all is what it seems.

Her boots and heavy socks and the wool leg-
gings which she hated but which her mother
always made her wear weighted her down,
and the shock of the sudden cold numbed
her. Even so with effort she was able to half
wade, half scramble, over the submerged
cranberry vines toward shore as the ice contin-
ued to give way before her.

Pudges stood on the shore with his paws
planted in the dead grass. Head tilted to one
side, he looked at her with a quizzical expression.

So...the little girl is not drowning after all. She seems
able to save herself. At this point, it *seems*, the reader's only real
worry is the nature of the man running toward her. But didn't
we just remind ourselves that all may not be what it seems?

This may be the perfect place for the author to ratchet
up the suspense. Let's see how it's done:

She had nearly reached the safety of the slope that bordered the bog, and was in fact preparing an impassioned defense against the licking she was sure to receive upon returning home soaked and chilled to the bone, when she stepped off the vines into an irrigation ditch and sank in over her head. Holding her breath, she struggled to reach the surface but found that she had drifted beneath the ice, which formed a hard, unyielding carapace above her. The more she pounded with her fists to break through, the more she slipped away from the opening her body had created. Involuntarily, she opened her mouth to gasp for breath, and as she did so her lungs began to fill with water.

Another twist! Another reversal of fortune! Just when it seems as though the child will make it to shore, she plunges deeper, slides under the ice, and begins to drown. Meanwhile the man is running towards her. A number of conflicting questions should now be paramount with the reader. Will our little girl drown? Will she manage to reach shore on her own? If not, will the man reach her in time to save her? If he reaches her in time, will he pull her to shore—only to harm her?

At this point the Prologue has come to an abrupt end—with, using a classic device of the silent cinema, a **cliffhanger**. Is there a reader who, having come this far, will not continue on to Chapter One, to learn the outcome?

Surprise!

Okay, so the reader, having accepted the bait, is hooked. Now you, the writer, can just sit back and, like an angler reeling in an exhausted fish, let the story unravel itself, right?

Wrong. Writing—to switch metaphors—is like driving an automobile. Just because you've started the engine and have steered the car onto the road doesn't mean you can relax and turn your attention to other matters. The day of automatic pilots for automobiles may lie somewhere in the near future, but it hasn't arrived yet. Operating an automobile requires your full attention; more than that—your constant vigilance, not to mention the conscientious application of all your driving skills.

So, too, it is with writing.

Now, where were we? Ah, yes: Chapter One—which you can think of as Chapter Two, if you wish, which is the number it would have been had I chosen to call the Prologue "Chapter One." The important consideration here is that the reader has finished the first chapter, or unit, and has proceeded on to the second.

In the old movie serials of the silent era (and in the golden age of talkies), each episode, as we mentioned above, ended with a cliffhanger. The following week's episode would resume where the previous week's left off. Our heroine, pursued by villains (whose intentions are anything but honorable), has plunged over the cliff's sheer edge. The last we see of her, she is frantically grasping with outstretched hand at a fragile tree limb; even as we gasp in horror the limb begins to slowly, inexorably give way. There can be no doubt that our heroine is about to plummet to her death.

There the episode comes to an abrupt halt. Next week, as the new installment opens (after a brief recapitulation of the scene where she topples over the edge), we see her miraculously saved. How, by what or by whom, doesn't matter. She is saved—just so that she can be placed into immediate peril again. (One of the most popular of these serials was aptly titled *The Perils of Pauline.*) At the end of this episode, there will be another cliffhanger. This time, perhaps, she will be swept by a swift current over a precipitous waterfall; or she will be tied to railroad tracks as a speeding train approaches. Or about to be pounced upon and devoured by a ferocious lion or other beast. Or—well (if you'll forgive the pun), you get the picture.

The cliffhanger can be a powerful device, and should be employed in most, if not all, mysteries. No less a genius than Charles Dickens used it to good effect, in the days when most novels appeared first in magazines, in installments, before they were bound in book form. But the cliffhanger should be used sparingly, or better yet, unobtrusively, that is to say, subtly; else you run the risk of producing a mere **potboiler**—a poorly written novel, totally lacking in literary worth, produced as quickly as possible for profit. We—you and I, dear reader—no matter how meager our talents, aspire to do better than that, don't we?

We'll talk more about cliffhangers, and their proper use, when we get to **pacing**.

Right now let's direct our attention to something we've thus far shamefully neglected, namely **story**: *the sequence of events as they happen.* The need for story in a mystery should be obvious; after all, isn't story what the book—any work of fiction—is all about? I mention story only so that I can define what is meant by the next essential, namely plot.

Plot is *the sequence in which the author presents or arranges the events of the story.* A mystery novel seldom, if ever, begins at the beginning. It often begins at the end—of the victim's life. The actual story may have begun days or months or even years earlier, when victim and murderer first met, perhaps. Or when a certain decision was made, whatever that may have been: to steal a painting, to cheat on one's spouse, to drive while intoxicated, to ridicule someone, to move into a certain neighborhood.

In this respect, in plotting a mystery novel you must work backwards. You begin with a murder, then work back to earlier events to show how the murder came about. You can do this with **flashbacks**—scenes that are inserted to show events that occurred at an earlier time. (Flashbacks can be tricky; if not done adroitly they can come across as contrived.) Or you can move backwards by summarizing with dialogue—a character simply describes to another character an event that occurred on a previous occasion. The character may have been a witness to such an event. Or he or she (a clever detective, let us say) may simply reconstruct what, given the nature of the evidence, must have occurred. You, the author, also "work backwards" in that, knowing the identity of the murderer, and the events that led to the murder, you must plan scenes so that necessary clues—as well as red herrings (false clues)—are planted.

Incidentally, in choosing to begin *Marmalade and Murder* with a Prologue, I was able to show prior events (*prior* to the murder) in proper chronological order, thus avoiding the use of flashback.

Hold it! What about the little girl? The last we saw of her she had fallen through the ice and was drowning. How can you, the author, be so callous as to forget all about her?

The answer, of course, is that I have not forgotten the little girl at all. I deliberately left her wedged under the ice. In doing so I compel the reader to turn the page to the next chapter to learn the child's fate.

Eagerly (one hopes) the reader, breathless, flips the page and encounters this:

> Following directions she had printed earlier
> off the Internet, Cheryl Fernandes drove down
> a vaguely familiar road until she came to a
> makeshift sign tacked to a tree.

Wait a minute! What's going on here? Who is this Cheryl Fernandes? Who gives a hoot about directions printed off the Internet? What happened to the little girl?

We read on:

> A bold black arrow beneath the words AUC-
> TION PREVIEW pointed toward an open-
> ing in the woods. Obeying the arrow, she
> turned from the pavement onto a gravel
> track that took her through a copse of
> mixed deciduous and evergreen trees out
> to a cranberry bog and onto an earthen
> dike.

What, for Pete's sake, has any of this to do with what came before? True, there is mention of a cranberry bog; perhaps this woman, this Cheryl Fernandes, will happen upon the scene in time to save the drowning child? Or perhaps she'll arrive too late, but will at least discover the body? Or could it be that she will witness something important, such as a man furtively running into the woods?

Soon, however, despite our expectations we realize that this chapter is concerned, not with little girls drowning beneath the ice, but with the preview for an estate auction to be held the following day. Gradually, we shift (or the skillful author shifts) our attention to the present action. This woman, this Cheryl Fernandes, seems somewhat preoccupied; we wonder what her interest in the auction might be. Then, two or three pages into the chapter, just when we are beginning to forget all about the little girl, we are shocked (if that is not too strong a word) by the following:

> Such peace, such beauty, gave the lie to the murder that had been committed only yards away from where she stood.

So that's it, the perceptive reader exclaims. The little girl has been murdered after all, most likely at the hands of the man whom she spotted running toward her. The author, by keeping us in suspense, has spared us the gory details.

Not so! we soon learn. The author has spared us nothing—because there was nothing to spare. We—the perceptive reader—have been grossly deceived. Gradually, the author imparts the following information: one, the murder took place inside the house; two, the victim was an adult male; three, this woman, this Cheryl Fernandes, is none other than the little girl, all grown up. The "drowning" incident happened thirty-six years earlier.

This thirty-six-year gap accounts for giving the title Prologue to what might otherwise have been Chapter One. Though the reader may at first feel mildly deceived, he or she eventually learns that the events of the past are closely connected with the murder.

❖

There is neither time nor space to adequately show examples of the many devices I used in Chapter One of *Marmalade and Murder* to keep the reader's interest directed toward the action on hand, while at the same time revealing pertinent information about the past. Dialogue was one device; conflict another. And of course I attempted to maintain a sense of mystery by hinting at this, that, or the other. Without further revelations from *Marmalade and Murder* (there may be readers curious enough to want to read the book on their own; it wouldn't be fair to divulge too much), we'll take a close look at the various devices and techniques (call them tricks if you will) at the author's disposal, along with all the other ingredients necessary to writing a successful mystery novel.

Something Smells Fishy

When planning the writing of a mystery novel, a question you must ask yourself from the very beginning is, what will make this story—this plot—this novel—unique? Hundreds of mysteries are published each year—how will this one be different? How will you make yours stand out from all the others?

Will the ending come as a surprise? A surprise ending is not an absolute necessity. But it is highly desirable.

Or will the primary interest lie somewhere else—for instance, in the background? This is not to imply that background, or setting—**local color** if you please—will, all by itself, salvage a novel that suffers from a humdrum story or clumsy plotting or insipid characters or pedestrian writing—but many an author has achieved success by relying, in part, on exotic or colorful settings to cause the reader to overlook, or forgive, what might otherwise be glaring flaws or weaknesses.

In any event, the plot should, to some extent, be character-driven. In the golden age of mystery novels—in the 1920's especially—the emphasis was on the puzzle, the ingenious plot. Characters were often little more than stick figures, wooden representations; they existed only for the sake of the clever plot. This was the era when locked-room mysteries—the so-called impossible crime—were popular.

Modern readers, on the other hand, are likely to be more interested in the characters themselves, in their motivations (as opposed to **motive**, which is something else entirely), in the psychology behind their actions. That is, they expect the plot to be organic—they expect it to grow out of the characters, and not be imposed on them from the outside (i.e., that it not be contrived by you, the omnipotent author; that your characters not be puppets on a string).

❖

Another decision you will have to face, once you have an inkling as to story and plot, is whether to **outline** or not.

The answer to this one is entirely up to you. Some writers need to know what is going to happen at every step of the way. This technique can work very well when it comes to such devices as foreshadowing and the planting of clues. But even these writers, the ones who rely on outlines, will have to be flexible; the characters, if well developed, may have their own ideas as to what they will or will not do next. Besides it's very difficult to surprise your readers if you don't leave room to surprise yourself.

At this stage you may be wondering: what comes first, the chicken or the egg? Where does a story—a full-blown novel—come from? How does it all begin?

Some writers begin with an idea, or a vague notion, or an image, or a catchy title, or a character about whom they wish to learn more. Sometimes a sentence, or just a phrase, will pop into your head and insist on being developed into a story, or an essay, or a poem, or even (heaven help you!) a novel.

When writing a mystery, however, you should at least know the ending to your story. And you probably should know the identity of the murderer from the outset. That last statement may seem obvious, but there are writers who will create a mystery in which a murder occurs for which there are any number of suspects, all of them equals: each has a compelling reason for wanting the victim dead; each has had an opportunity to commit the crime; each has a plausible alibi. The clues, however ambiguous, point equally to each as being, or not being, the culprit.

This type of mystery can be risky; if towards the end the author arbitrarily picks one of the suspects and makes him or her the murderer, the reader may feel manipulated or even cheated—unless, of course, the author produces some sort of brilliant ending, or pulls off some other trick, or shows that it only *seemed* as though the suspects were equal, whereas the clues were there all along that pointed to Miss Jones as the ax-murderer. So, to reiterate: you probably should know from the outset who the murderer is. And how the crime was committed. And how the detective will solve it.

Did I mention the word **detective**?

Every mystery novel needs a detective—someone to go about gathering clues or otherwise solving the crime.

Did I mention the word **crime**? I might just as well have written **murder**. For almost invariably—not one hundred percent of the time, but close to it—the mystery novel is about the unlawful killing of a fellow human being. There's something about the ultimate foul deed, about the precipitous dispatch of a living, breathing person into the Great Beyond, that compels our attention more than any other crime. True, there have been successful mysteries which are concerned with the solution of lesser infractions. But these books are rare. Even if a mystery is ostensibly a spy novel, or about a gang of thieves who pull off a spectacular heist or some other caper, at least one violent death generally occurs.

The point bears repeating: mystery novels—whodunits—are not about just any criminal activity; they concern themselves with that gravest and most nefarious of all crimes, the murder of a human being. For whodunits are more than mere puzzles, to be marveled at and solved; they are, in effect, about the disruption of the social order. And they are about the eventual re-establishment of that order, with the apprehension and just punishment of the perpetrator.

Now, in order for the social order to be restored there must be an agent of retribution, i.e., a knight in shining armor.

Oh, hold on a second—silly me! Wrong genre! I was thinking Medieval Romance: you know, the kingdom being laid waste by a fire-breathing dragon; the only possible salvation, the sacrifice of a young damsel to appease the evil monster; the valiant knight riding forth to slay the dragon, and as his reward receiving the hand of the princess (for the damsel is not only a virgin, she is also the king's daughter).

But you can understand my mistake, can't you? For isn't the Medieval Romance, as described above, likewise about the disruption, and ultimate restoration, of the social order? And isn't the detective in the mystery novel really a modern-day knight in shining armor, albeit in disguise? True, he may be a she— and an elderly she at that; think of Agatha Christie's Miss Marple. And his armor might be somewhat tarnished; think of Raymond Chandler's Philip Marlow. He might even be an alcoholic, or a reformed criminal, or—well, let's not belabor the point.

The point being: you'll need a detective of some sort, male or female, young or old, of spotless character or hopelessly blemished, of whatever race or sexual orientation, to ride forth and slay the dragon; that is to say, to go around and poke his or her nose into various places, especially where it's not wanted (and perhaps in doing so get conked on the noggin); to fossick for clues; to sneak about and listen to clandestine conversations behind closed curtains; and to otherwise find out "whodunit"— who disrupted the social order by committing the capital crime of murder.

An entire book, I suppose, could be (and for all I know has been) written on types of detectives. Since this book, the one you're presently reading, is more overview than instruction manual, I'll just run through some of the more familiar variations.

First off, the kind of mystery I've been describing is (more or less) the so-called **cozy**. This genteel variation of the genre derives its name from the tea cozy (or *cosy*, to give it its proper British spelling), the knitted or padded covering for a teapot, the purpose of which is to keep the tea hot—or perhaps I should say warm, hot being perhaps too intense for the classic cozy mystery.

In the archetypal cozy (the mystery novel, not the covering), violence is seldom graphic; in fact, the murder, or murders, frequently occur offstage. The body of Sir William, stabbed through the heart, or possibly shot through the head, is found by the maid, or the butler, or one of the guests, lying face down on the floor of the library. The library, of course, is that of a manor house in the remote English countryside, though it could also be a mansion or *pied-à-terre* in the heart of London. Various guests, along with family members and servants, are there for the weekend, any number of whom might possibly want to see Sir William dead.

There are countless variations on the theme, of course. Sir William may not obviously have been murdered. It may at first appear that he suffered a heart attack, or died as the result of an accidental fall, until a medical examiner, or coroner (or better yet, an amateur sleuth) determines otherwise. Or it may very well be Sir William's twin brother lying dead on the library floor. Or—ghastly thought!—the body may be so disfigured (charred from having been in a fire, though in this instance, unless the head fell into the fireplace, the body will more likely be found lying outside in a copse) that it is mistaken for that of

Sir William, while in actuality being that of someone else entirely.

(Now there's a title for a mystery novel: *The Corpse in the Copse!*)

In any event, in the classic cozy the sundry characters find themselves confined within a more or less limited space—in a manor house, or on an isolated farm, or in a tiny village, or aboard a ship or a train or even an airplane, or on a small island. An inspector from Scotland Yard may be called in to solve the case, but more often one of the guests, or townspeople—an amateur— assumes the role of detective. In the final scene, the detective, of whatever stripe, assembles the suspects into one room, and reveals the identity of the murderer, preferably by subterfuge, i.e., by tricking the murderer into revealing him- or herself.

To recapitulate: in the cozy, the detective (the person who actually solves the crime, as opposed to any bumbling official assigned to do so) is, if not the local constable or an inspector sent by Scotland Yard (there exist, of course, American counterparts for cozies set on this side of the Atlantic)—if the detective is not an official policeman, or some other person in authority, then he or she is an amateur, of whatever social standing—Lord or scullery maid or maiden aunt or parish priest.

Incidentally, you may have noticed that from time to time I qualify a statement with a phrase such as "more or less," "perhaps," or the like. This is to remind myself, as well as you, dear reader, that (have I said this before?) there are hundreds, if not thousands, of ways that a mystery novel can deviate from the "norm."

My own humble effort—*Marmalade and Murder*—while acknowledging the British cozy, also pays homage to its more gritty American cousin. True, the initial murder takes place offstage, as do one or two subsequent killings. (I'm being coy here, so as not to give too much away.) But in the course of events some bloodshed occurs onstage. And there are elements of (nail-biting I hope) suspense, as well as—dare I say it? a modicum of romance (tied up with the suspense, of course). And humor. Quite a bit of humor.

And the denouement is anything but conventional.

But—as the recently published author said, over a glass of wine, to his girlfriend on their first date: "Enough about *me*. Let's talk about my book."

In the matter of detectives, I resolved on two: both amateurs, one reluctant, the other eccentric.

Every Sherlock Holmes has his Watson—who, among other things, serves as a foil. Holmes is clever—almost fiendishly so; an absolute genius. Watson, solidly English—courageous, honest, and loyal to a fault—is, to put it bluntly, rather stolid if not downright dull. Not dull-witted, mind you; he is after all a doctor. But he can at times be, shall we say, somewhat obtuse—at least when it comes to solving crimes. In most (but not all) of the Sherlock Holmes stories he functions as narrator; it is he who, through recollection and reminiscence recounts the story. More important, though, he asks questions (and thereby saves the reader the embarrassment of having to do so), giving Holmes the opportunity to explain, as well as display, his brilliant deductions.

The Usual Miscreants

Whatever your choice of detective(s), you'll want to otherwise people your novel (or short-story) with well-rounded, believable **characters**. Avoid flat stick figures, or "types." Each person in your story should be an individual. Each should have his or her own unique personality. Each should have one or two readily identifiable traits: a physical characteristic, perhaps, or a manner of speaking—something you can use from time to time to remind your readers that this is character A and not Character C. But don't overdo the quirks—you don't want to populate your fictional world with a bunch of eccentrics; you are after all writing a mystery, not a farce.

You want your characters to drive the plot. You want them to surprise you. (How else can you surprise the reader?)

Before we talk about the various roles these (as yet unnamed) characters will be called upon to play, we have to answer a question that may be bugging some of you: where are these characters to be found—these individuals, these men and women (and, yes, sometimes children and even animals), these animated beings who will perform the varied tasks which you, the almighty author, are about to impose upon them? Tasks such as loving and hating and lusting and fearing and lying and killing and dying and solving crimes—do we call Central Casting or the local Employment Agency?

Or do we use our imagination?

And what the hell is imagination?

Well, I can't answer that last question, except to remind you about *what if...*

But I can answer the question that came before it: yes, we do use our imagination (our *what if...*) to find the characters we'll need for our mystery. Did I say *find*? Perhaps I meant *create*? Or both. We find characters by creating them. We create characters by finding them. (I can hear you muttering amongst yourselves: *Find by creating? Create by finding? The man's talking in circles. Perhaps he is, indeed, dancing mad. Perhaps he hath, indeed, been bitten by the tarantula. Oh, where is Dubious Reader now that we need him?*)

Allow me to explain.

You'll find some of your characters already made to order: people you know, people you've met. You may even be related to one or two of them! All you need do now is to describe them, and then put your *what if...* to work. What if my lazy, good-for-nothing_____(Fill in the blank: next-door neighbor, brother-in-law, niece, wife's cousin, whoever)—what if he or she_____(Fill in the blank: poisoned his wife, was arrested for possessing drugs, embezzled from her employer, murdered the man who molested him as a child, whatever).

There are caveats, of course. If you're going to model a character on a real person, it's better if that person is already dead; that way he or she won't be in a position to sue you for libel. Model your villains on people you remember from your childhood, people who have long departed this mortal coil. Or use real persons only for minor characters—minor characters whom you favorably portray. Yet even here there's risk; your idea of a favorable portrayal may be someone else's idea of a derogatory (read *libelous*) description.

So, maybe using real persons as characters for your work of fiction isn't such a good idea. And if not real persons, then what?

Not to fear. What you do is, well, sort of what Dr. Frankenstein did: you create characters the way he created his monster, by gathering pieces (though you're not limited to just body parts; you can use personality and character traits as well) from various sources and putting them together into something new. That brother-in-law you despise? Borrow the way he walks with a stoop, and combine it with your wife's cousin's bad breath. Add your next-door neighbor's predilection for wearing tight-fitting jeans, and your seventh-grade teacher's flaming red hair, and…lo! you've created not a monster, but a plausible murderer.

One for whom you won't be sued.

Though, again, a caveat. No matter how imaginary your characters, no matter how unconnected they may be to any persons living or dead, there's always someone who's going to come up to you and say, "You can't fool me; you obviously modeled so and so on me." And nothing—*nothing*—you say or do will ever convince that person otherwise.

Characters are where you find them. That is to say, characters are where you create them. They're composites. Now, in truth, the best characters are those which you do not consciously "put together." The best characters arise from the subconscious. Or from the unconscious. *They* are based on *your* experience of the world. But that, dear reader, is a truth which you will eventually learn for yourself, if, following my advice, you sit down and write. And write. And (yes) write.

Perhaps one or two final words on the subject are in order:

Do not model your characters on other fictional characters—people you've read about in books. Doing so will result only in cardboard characters, or characters who are flat and unconvincing. And do not model them on people you see on television or in the movies. These people are already cardboard;

they don't need you to apply an additional coating of paint.

But now for the real secret (already hinted at); the title of this book promises secrets, so I suppose I have to share one with you now and then. The real secret to creating great characters is *to base them on yourself*. We are, every one of us, Everyman. We are all, potentially, clever detectives. We are also, equally potentially, evil murderers. We are policemen, and thieves; cowards, and heroes; sinners, and saints. You want characters? Look into your heart, into your very soul, and write.

What if you wished somebody dead…

What if somebody—somebody detestable, somebody without any redeeming virtues—stood in your way, was the sole obstacle to your achieving the happiness, the success, the love, that you fervently desire, that you so richly deserve? Imagine yourself a murderer. How would *you* go about disposing of that hated person? How would *you* attempt to cover your tracks? Then imagine yourself the detective charged with solving the crime. Imagine yourself an innocent suspect. Or the grieving spouse of the victim. How would *you* react? To grief? To guilt? To terror?

See, it's that easy.

❖

Now let's take a breather, and review some of the roles the various characters must assume.

We've already discussed the need for one or more detectives. The word *sleuth* derives, through Middle English, from an Old Norse word meaning "track of an animal." Sleuthhounds, or bloodhounds, are noted for their remarkable tracking ability. Their very name invokes images of desperate criminals, escaped convicts perhaps, scrambling with frantic haste across treacherous moors, or crashing through dense forest land, all the while glancing fearfully behind as the relentless baying of their canine pursuers draws ever nearer. No wonder, then, that the word *sleuth* has become synonymous with *detective*.

Whether your fictional detective possesses the keen nose—and tenacity—of a bloodhound, or is someone reluctantly thrust (by circumstances) into the role and only halfheartedly stumbles through to the end, or falls into some other category altogether, depends entirely on you—on what type of mystery novel you are writing.

I mentioned earlier that I chose as my sleuths two amateur detectives, one eccentric, the other reluctant. Lena Lombardi, the eccentric one, leads the chase; for her it is largely a game, a way to ease loneliness and boredom. Cheryl Fernandes, the reluctant one, allows herself—partly through friendship for Lena, partly out of a sense of obligation to the victim—to be led. This "device" (of leader and led) provided all sorts of advantages. For one, it allowed me to play off one character against the other. Every novel needs **conflict** (more about that later; for now I'll just touch upon the subject). Having Cheryl feel herself tugged by Lena in directions she didn't particularly want to go allowed for interesting conflict, both inner (within Cheryl) and outer (between the two women).

For another, the device allowed me to put the amateur sleuths into situations that two women would not normally expect to find themselves—breaking into a house late at night, for example, or in imminent danger of being deliberately run over by an automobile, or—well, once again I'll leave off in the middle of a sentence so as not to reveal too much to potential readers of *Marmalade and Murder*. Suffice it to say that, with two such diverse characters, I was able to come up with a variety of suspenseful situations.

Dialogue was a third advantage; having a pair of characters in frequent disagreement with one another not only allowed for dramatic dialogue, but also provided a way for me, the author, to give, by means of the many conversations between Lena and Cheryl, information necessary for the reader to know and understand. For example, at critical stages throughout the novel the two women discuss the crimes (there are several of course, murder and lesser felonies), possible motives, various suspects, the aptitude (or ineptitude) of the authorities, potential courses of action, the wisdom (or lack of it) in continuing their investigation, and any number of other matters of vital interest that must be dealt with by the author in one way or another.

A great deal more can—and no doubt will—be said about detectives. For now, the point to bear in mind is that you must choose your detective wisely. He, she, or they must fit not only the type of mystery you're writing (cozy, thriller, police procedural, etc.) but also your individual style—and abilities. For example, whole series have been written about blind detectives. It's a great idea—but one which requires special knowledge, or extraordinary imagination, to carry off successfully (i.e., convincingly.) And whole series have been written featuring detectives who never venture outside their house. It's a great gimmick—if you can manage it. The "secret," then, is to think the matter through: choose a detective with whom you feel comfortable, and who will best showcase *your* talents.

What's that you say? All of this is obvious? I'm flogging a dead horse? Everyone knows the importance of choosing the right sort of detective?

Okay, buddy, I'll move on to the next subject. (But don't come along later asking *me* to explain about detectives!)

Next we'll talk about the **victim**. Every murder mystery requires at least one. (And right now I've got a prime candidate for the job. Exactly what do you mean, Mr. Dubious Reader Number Two, by accusing me of "flogging a dead horse"? What do you say to flogging a dead body—yours!)

Come, come, Mr. Lodi. There's no need to fly off the handle. Threatening readers is most unseemly behavior in an author of your distinction.

Don't patronize me, please! Or attempt to flatter me with "author of your distinction." (Or are you attempting sarcasm?) I'm not "flying off the handle." I've remained quite calm, when you consider the provocation! Besides, I'm threatening only one of my readers—the one who's acting the part of a wisenheimer.

Where was I? Oh yes, the victim.

Questions which you must ask yourself: What is the victim's relationship to the murderer? To the other characters? Why would anyone want this person dead? The classic mystery often features a victim with many enemies—hence, a plethora of suspects, each with his or her own motive for committing the foul deed. Conversely, the victim may have been a pillar of the community, beloved of all. Or an innocent child. Here, the mystery to be solved is not only whodunit, but also why?

One victim leads to another, of course. That is to say, in mystery novels—the kind you are contemplating—the killer often strikes a second time, usually for the purpose of silencing a possible witness to the first murder, or eliminating someone with incriminating knowledge. And even then the bodies may continue to pile up; before the initial crime is solved any number of folks may have met an untimely end.

As I stated earlier, there is no standard recipe for writing a murder mystery; there are only standard ingredients—each with inexact measurements. How many victims will your novel require? That is for you to decide. Or rather, for your characters to decide for you; for if you are at all serious about writing, you will (having no real choice in the matter) let your characters—most of the time, at least—have their own way.

The notion of having a crass murderer dictate to you what happens next may rankle, but such is the nature of things. It may well be, too, that the murderer is him- or herself helpless; other characters may act in such a way that they demand (from the standpoint of the murderer) to be killed—i.e., to become victims themselves.

Another statement I made earlier was something to the effect that you must write your book twice—the first time forward, the second time backwards. Really, though, you are always working backwards. You have been advised, after all, to choose your detective before any crime has been committed! And you are being urged to come up with a victim (possibly with others to follow) before you have decided upon the identity of your murderer. You may even have a number of suspects—though I do not advise this—before you know which one of them is guilty.

Are all novels written this way?

No. You can begin most novels with nothing more than a set of characters, as few as one or two, and a dilemma perhaps, or a life-threatening situation, or nothing more than a character trait or vague notion—and let them work things out. You need have no idea how the story will end. Or what will happen along the way.

Not so with the mystery.

❖

So, moving forward—that is to say, backward—we now come to the question of **suspects**. One of whom (prepare for the drum roll!) may even be the murderer.

What's this? you ask. One of the suspects *may be* the murderer? What nonsense is this? Of course the actual murderer must be found among the suspects. Common sense dictates...

[I'm shaking my head.] No. Common sense does not dictate; the actual murderer is not necessarily one of the suspects. Part of the fun of writing a mystery is fooling the reader; part of the fun of reading a mystery is being fooled—so long as the fooling is done fairly. We'll come to the matter of **the least likely suspect** shortly.

For now, suffice it to say that you will need a number of suspects: at least three or four, though probably no more than six or seven. Each should have a plausible reason—a motive— for wanting the victim dead. Each should have an opportunity to commit the crime. And each should have an alibi—or none should have an alibi. Or some should, and others shouldn't.

You see, the variations are endless. That is one of the reasons, no doubt, for the continuing popularity of the mystery novel, which has been around, now, for about a century and a half.

As I hinted (rather broadly) above, your list of suspects does not have to include the actual culprit. You can throw your reader—your armchair sleuth—off the scent by creating a number of suspects, some with more appearance of guilt than others, but none of whom is actually guilty of any crime. Or one or two may be guilty of a crime—such as blackmail, or theft, or withholding or destroying evidence, or what have you—but not the capital crime of murder. In other words, you heap suspicion upon any- and everyone—except the guilty party.

Now, the convention of the least likely suspect (the person whom no one suspects at all) turning out to be the murderer is not a new one. It dates back to when—well, probably to when mystery novels as we know them first began to appear, in the latter half of the nineteenth century. So the perceptive reader—and you may very well, with justification, so designate yourself (everyone except *you*, O Dubious One; you know who you are!)—the perceptive reader is already wise to the trick. And the writers of mysteries know that the readers are wise. And the readers know that the writers know that the readers...

You can see for yourself where it all leads. When reading a mystery, you should always look for the innocuous, the innocent-seeming, character. The one who appears to be serving no real purpose—who could have been left out, without harm to the story (or so it seems). That person might very well be the murderer. Or, that person might very well not be the murderer. The author may have included this character for the sole purpose of deceiving you into thinking, "This person, whom nobody has cause to suspect, will most likely turn out to be the one everybody should have suspected in the first place."

The one thing you must do, regardless of how many suspects you include, or how you present them, is to introduce the murderer early on—preferably in the first few chapters, or at least in the first third of the book. It won't do to have your murderer appear out of the blue, as it were, in the final chapter, with little or no preparation (for the reader) on your part. Introduce the culprit as soon—and as unobtrusively—as you are able. That way, when the reader finishes the book, he or she will look back and think, ah, I should have suspected Sir Humphrey all along!

❖

Speaking of culprits—you'll need a **motive**. Perhaps I should rephrase that last statement—I can, in my inner ear, hear Dubious Reader smirking.

Smirking? You can hear me smirking? And just what sort of sound, Mr. Lodi, does a person make when he or she smirks?

Ah, you've got me there, D. R. Chalk one up for you—though in all honesty I undoubtedly would have caught, and corrected, that minor lapse in my very first revision of this chapter. (I cannot emphasize too much the importance of carefully reading, and rereading, for the purpose of rewriting, every word, every syllable, every punctuation mark, that you put on paper or screen.) Anyhow, I can, in my inner ear, *picture* Dubious Reader smirking: I'll *need a motive?* [he asks, with a smirk] My *motive for writing a mystery novel is to make money. Or to achieve fame. Or perhaps both.*

So I'll rephrase that opening sentence to, "Speaking of culprits, you'll want to make sure that your murderer has a plausible motive for committing the crime. Regardless of what that motive is, it must "ring true" with the reader. I say this, because in devising your little mystery novel you may come up with a brilliant idea, or any number of brilliant ideas, for hiding clues or surprising the reader, for colorful characters, for a unique setting, or for a novel way of killing someone (a new type of poison, let us say) or for disposing of the murder weapon, or for any number of things—and then, at the last minute, as if it were an afterthought, tack on the motive.

And who knows? You may get away with it—with bestowing upon your culprit a weak or unconvincing motive; the sheer brilliance of your other ideas may blind most readers to the fact that the reason you give your killer for willfully taking the life of another human being doesn't quite fit the bill—seems rather contrived; like something you might find in a book, but never in real life.

Regardless of what your other considerations may be, you must, fairly early on, wrestle with the problem of motive(s): Why did the murderer commit the crime? What motivates the other characters? What do they have to gain? to hide? to protect?

Now, your murderer's motive may be something as mundane as a desire for monetary gain—to steal something of value, to inherit wealth, to get rid of a business rival. Or it could be for love (or lust). Or jealousy. Or revenge. Or to achieve a political goal—to eliminate a liberal, or a conservative, in power. It might even be an altruistic motive: to right an unforgivable wrong perpetrated upon another; or to save an innocent person from suffering grievous harm at the hands of someone evil—or perceived to be evil—(whom your killer eliminates by violent means); or to save a pristine wilderness from being destroyed by greedy developers.

If you choose an obvious motive, such as monetary gain, you may, as we've seen, wish to hide the identity of the real culprit by presenting several other characters with equally powerful motives. Or you may conceal the true motive for the crime by making it appear to be something else. In doing this, you may even enlist the aid of your killer—he or she murders out of a desire for revenge, but makes it appear as though the victim died as a result of a robbery.

One final note: if you feel especially clever, you may even devise (notice my choice of word here: *devise* rather than *write* or *create*; I'm being coy) you may devise a mystery novel based on motive—where the ultimate interest lies in *why* the murder was committed, rather than how or by whom.

A Minor Detour

To forestall any possible adverse criticisms from my old pal, Dubious Reader (and if he—I'm convinced it's a he; he's jealous, that's what he is, wishes it were he who was writing this book, thinks he could do a better job of it—is ever found murdered, you won't have far to seek for a motive, nor for the obvious Prime Suspect, though I assure you that that Prime Suspect will have an ironclad alibi), let me admit that this chapter is something of a hodgepodge. Now, to be honest, if I really thought it was a hodgepodge I'd rewrite it, wouldn't I? Let us therefore refer to it as a miscellany. In it, I lump together a number of topics, two of them specific to the mystery genre, the others pertinent to any form of fiction (and in some cases, nonfiction).

What is a chapter, anyhow? The earliest manuscripts—scrolls—not only were not divided into chapters, they were not even sectioned off into paragraphs. Worse, they contained no punctuation, nor were there upper-, as distinguished from lower-, case letters. The reader sort of had to guess where one sentence let off and another began. This not only made reading more tedious than it ought to be, it led to confusion, since there were many instances where the author's intended meaning was obscured.

Nowadays, sentences are essential to convey meaning; paragraphs are useful, if for nothing else, than to give the reader (we'll make this one a she) a chance to pause and rest her eyes—and find the place where she left off when she resumes reading.

Likewise, dividing books into chapters is only a convenience for the reader. And an encouragement. Confronted with a five-hundred page novel, with no chapter breaks, which one of us might not feel disinclined to begin reading? "Five hundred pages? Are you kidding? I've only got one lifetime," the wary (or weary) reader says to herself. But break that same novel into, say, thirty chapters, and the reader thinks, "These chapters aren't very long; I'll read one or two tonight, and maybe a couple more tomorrow." Suddenly the book doesn't seem long, at all.

In the past, authors (or their editors) might divide a lengthy work into only a small number of chapters. This paucity of sectional breaks worked, in Victorian times for example, when people had more leisure to read than they do today. (That is to say, folks took time to read, and were not distracted by the many gadgets and diversions available to us in this so-called modern era.) In those days most readers seemed actually to prefer a leisurely pace; they had the whole evening ahead of them, or were snowbound for the day, or had a cozy nook by the fireplace or comfortable hammock under a tree, and looked forward to sinking themselves into a good, long read.

Modern readers, on the other hand, demand a decidedly quicker pace. Authors and editors know that dividing a book into very short chapters can make the action (whether in a novel or a work of nonfiction) seem to move along more rapidly. A lot more seems to be happening than would be the case were the chapters longer. This may be a mere illusion, or it may be because the author has skillfully paced the action so that the ending of each chapter makes the reader want to turn the page, to see what happens next. But, to reiterate, the seemingly quicker pace of shorter chapters may only be an illusion.

Smaller chapters can make a short book seem longer, since there's all that extra space, both at the top of the chapter heading, and at the end of the chapter. A two-hundred page novel divided into short chapters will "read" more quickly than one of similar length divided into only a few long chapters.

You can, of course, alternate between short and long chapters. Just how you divide your book into chapters depends on what you are attempting to achieve, in matters of pacing, and in such matters as suspense or atmosphere.

I wasn't being totally frank when I said that chapters are primarily a convenience for readers. They can also, especially in works of nonfiction, such as this one, be a means of ordering material in a systematic and logical sequence.

Systematic and logical? Surely, Mr. Lodi, you jest.

Okay, I'll admit I got sidetracked. This chapter was supposed to have been about various and sundry other things. But you know, no aspect of writing is unimportant. If by getting sidetracked I've made you, the reader, more aware of the importance of space (as well as the positioning of text) in a piece of writing, I will not have wasted my, nor your, time.

Various and Sundry

Okay, no more digressions, I promise (for now, anyhow).

Returning to our recipe for mysteries, let's consider an ingredient already mentioned but only partially defined: the **red herring**. Come to think of it, red herrings might more appropriately have been included in the chapter titled "Something Smells Fishy." Herrings are a type of fish which, when smoked, turn a reddish color. They're quite tasty. They're also quite smelly. They were used—I'm not sure under what circumstances—to divert hounds from the scent of whatever it was they were tracking.

But you can see it, can't you, in your mind's eye: not overly bright hounds snuffling along with eager noses to the ground, suddenly catching a whiff of red herrings that have been tossed in the area, and with boomful baying veering off to investigate? If these hounds were anything like some of the dogs I've known, upon coming upon the herrings they either devoured them then and there, or if the fish were, from advanced decomposition, particularly odoriferous, they flung themselves gleefully onto their backs and rolled about in the mess until they, too, were abundantly fragrant.

Actual red herrings were smoked fish used to throw hounds (sleuths) off the scent; literary red herrings are false or misleading clues used to distract detectives (sleuths)—as well as readers—from discovering the real facts of the case.

In plotting your mystery you'll want to include any number of red herrings. You, the author, will plant most of these false clues. But you may wish to enlist the aid of your culprit, or even one of the other characters; murderers have been known to plant their own red herrings, to deceive or confuse the detective; and secondary characters have been known to do likewise, for example when they hope to protect someone who they believe may be guilty. From the reader's perspective, it makes no difference whether the false clues are planted directly by you, the author, or by one of the other characters acting as your agent. If planted skillfully, red herrings can trip up even the most skillful of detectives (and the most jaded of readers).

Planting of clues, false or real, leads to our next topic, **playing fair**.

In the Golden Age of the mystery, playing fair with the reader was a concept dear to the hearts of writers and their editors. For many aficionados, the chief pleasure to be derived from whodunits was the chance to outwit the detective, to solve the crime before he or she did. In that respect, a mystery novel was like a crossword puzzle; the author set up a situation, and following certain guidelines, provided characters and clues.

What were these guidelines?

First and foremost, all the information needed to solve the mystery must be presented. It's not fair to withhold essential facts. Nor is it fair for the detective to discover vital information behind the scenes (unless the reader has had an equal opportunity to so discover it), which he or she reveals only at the very end. And yet, the reader should not be able to easily guess the solution; but upon reading to the end, should think: *I should have guessed it!* This means that the author has to drop clues here and there—but unobtrusively. And should include a number of red herrings—false clues.

One way to place clues unobtrusively is to list them among nonclues. For example, the author describes a room, and in doing so mentions a number of objects: the scatter rug in front of the fireplace, an unusual lamp shade, a heavy glass ashtray, a collection of Indian arrowheads, a book on shade gardening. This is the home, incidentally, of a man named James Porter, a cousin of the murdered woman—her death from a heart attack has placed him second in line to inherit a vast fortune. Coincidentally, the first person in line to inherit (the only person to be standing in his way), also a cousin of James's, dies the following week, also, seemingly, of a heart attack.

Suspicious, the authorities order an autopsy on the second victim; finding traces of digitalis, they order the body of the first victim exhumed. Traces of digitalis are found in her, too.

So, what was the clue that was unobtrusively placed by the author in the description of the room? Why, the book on shade gardening, of course. Digitalis is found in foxgloves, a plant that tolerates shade; James, an avid gardener, had access to an ample supply of the beautiful but noxious flowers in his own back yard. The gardening book, by the way, does not lead directly to James as the murderer; it is just one of a number of clues which cause the reader, at the end, to exclaim, "All of the information needed to solve the mystery was there, all along."

Playing fair also means introducing the guilty person or persons early on—ideally, in the first few chapters. It's simply not cricket to introduce the murderer toward the end of the book. In the above scenario, James would have appeared early on, perhaps as one of the mourners at the funeral of his suddenly deceased cousin.

❖

In a roundabout way, playing fair leads to **point of view**—a subject which, since it is worthy of its own chapter, we'll reserve for discussion later.

In the meantime let's take a look at another of those ingredients which, on the surface, appear obvious. Every story has to occur somewhere, sometime. That is to say, every story requires a **setting**—a locale, or background against which the story takes place. Just as important as the physical setting is the temporal: the epoch or period in history, the season, even the time of day.

Setting may seem like a minor consideration—after all, what difference does it make where a story takes place? Shouldn't the emphasis be on the characters, or plot, or—if we're at the more literary end of the spectrum—the theme?

Not necessarily. I've already intimated that setting was a primary impetus for writing *Marmalade and Murder*. I know the cranberry bogs of southeastern Massachusetts intimately. I've used them effectively in ghost stories (*Moonlight Harvest*). I know their potential for creating atmosphere and suspense. Furthermore the bogs, though familiar territory to me, possess for many readers the allure of the exotic.

Setting can be an important factor in plotting; in *Marmalade and Murder* I arranged scenes and events in such a way (in other words, I plotted) so as to take full advantage of an isolated cranberry bog (and the surrounding woods and swamps) and an old screenhouse, both in the daytime and at night. To a lesser extent, to capture local color, I set several scenes on the coast of Cape Cod, with its beaches, birds, boats, and tides.

Setting, too, can be an important influence on characterization: initially on what sort of characters will inhabit a story, and subsequently on the development of those characters. A story set on the coast of Maine will feature different types of characters from a story set in the financial district of a large city. Weather and climate—both of which are elements of setting—can have a strong influence on characters and the way they act and interact.

Akin to setting, yet different from it, is **atmosphere**. The word derives from Latin; in its physical sense it refers to the "sphere of air" that surrounds us. In its literary sense, it refers to the air which we, as readers, breathe or feel (emotionally, psychologically, mentally) as we read. That air may be light and breezy, or heavy and oppressive, or something else entirely. Atmosphere is not quite the same as **mood**, but is close enough so that the two terms can be used more or less interchangeably.

Setting is a prime factor in the creation of atmosphere. A graveyard at midnight is sufficient unto itself to evoke fear and unease in the average reader. A rose garden on a sunny day no doubt brings forth in that same reader feelings of peace and beatitude. Add a solitary human figure to the graveyard, let us say a lost child, and fear and dread are intensified. Add two young lovers to the rose garden, and a romantic, perhaps an erotic, atmosphere prevails. Now add a hint of the uncanny to the graveyard—what appears to be a skeletal hand curving from behind a tombstone, or a luminous transparency issuing from the crevices of a mausoleum—and the atmosphere reeks with horror. As for the rose garden—introduce a venomous serpent, and you have, well, any number of possibilities.

Just how important atmosphere is to a work of fiction depends on what type of fiction, and on the author's purpose for writing it. In detective fiction, an air of suspense, of mystery (in the sense of bafflement), of unease, of danger, should predominate. There's room for levity and humor, of course. In fact, it's desirable to include lighter moments between the darker ones; sustained suspense, throughout an entire novel, is not only difficult to achieve, but also tiring. Readers need a moment now and then to pause and catch their breath. And it's precisely at such moments, when their guard is down, that you as author can hit them on the head with a new shock or surprise.

But that's a matter of **pacing**, which we'll discuss in a later chapter.

Conflict

A long time ago—in the 1970's—I lived alone and cooked my own meals. One of my favorite dishes, simple to prepare yet tasty and nutritious, consisted of canned tuna fish, Granny Smith apples, onions, curry, white wine, and perhaps one or two other ingredients, cooked in a skillet and served over brown rice. I must have been in a hurry one day, or under a great deal of stress (I was a social worker at the time, responsible for a number of difficult cases); I remember making the dish, wolfing the greater portion of it down, and storing the leftovers in the refrigerator. The odd thing is, the next day when I heated up the leftovers I discovered—belatedly—that I had in preparing the dish omitted the main ingredient, the tuna fish.

What I found striking, of course, was not that I forgot the tuna in the first place (as I said, I was preoccupied with other matters), but that on the day I made it I ate the meal—and evidently enjoyed it—without noticing the omission.

What does the above anecdote have to do with secrets and shortcuts for successful writing?

Just this: I almost, in writing this book, left out the tuna.

Now, that last statement is an exaggeration, made for dramatic effect. I didn't almost neglect to include the tuna—

the main ingredient—but I did nearly leave out one of the ingredients necessary for any work of fiction, and for many other
genres as well: **conflict**.

*Come now, Mr. Lodi, once again your memory seems to
have failed you—perhaps your mind is preoccupied? If you'll turn
back a dozen pages or so, you'll find that you did indeed, however
fleetingly, make reference to conflict.*

Ah, I've got you there, O Dubious One! I made that
earlier reference to conflict later—on the rewrite of that chapter—after I'd already composed this one.

*"Earlier." "Later." Surely you are, shall we say, confused,
Mr. Lodi? Disoriented. (Not, let us hope, a sign of dementia?) And
you hope to teach others how to write? Physician, heal thyself!*

In the above exchange [and below], albeit crudely, you
have an example of conflict in a work of nonfiction. Throughout this book, to engender interest (and a modicum of humor?),
I've included this running dialogue, this back-and-forth with
an imaginary, and disgruntled, quibbler whom I've dubbed
Dubious Reader. Doing so has allowed me, in a minor key, to
add drama to subjects that might otherwise border on the dull,
the drab, and the dreary.

*Such obtrusive alliteration: all those d's, Mr. Lodi—dia-
logue, disgruntled, dubbed, Dubious, Doing, drama, dull, drab,
dreary (not to mention the interior d's, as in border). It makes the
paragraph rather bumpy, wouldn't you say—sort of a washboard
effect, like driving along a rutted byway. You used to write much
better than this; you're showing signs of fatigue. Perhaps the stress of
writing this book is proving a bit too much for you.*

Leave alliteration (the repetition of initial sounds) out
of this! If I choose to discuss alliteration, I will do so in its

proper place—in the chapter dealing with poetry and verse. The topic being discussed in this chapter, in case you haven't noticed, is CONFLICT.

Temper, Mr. Lodi. Temper.

Despite its occasional use in nonfiction, conflict is more properly an element of fiction (as well as of drama). Conflict is what drives plots; they could hardly exist without it. Conflict—opposition, struggle—creates tension. It moves the plot forward.

Most stories have a chief character, a **protagonist**—sometimes referred to as the hero. Many stories also have an **antagonist**, the character who opposes the protagonist. If all this is Greek to you, well, that's because the terms come from the Greeks, who virtually invented drama. You want conflict? Read a tragedy written by Euripides or one of the other ancient Greek playwrights.

The character (or characters)—protagonist(s)—in any given story can be opposed by one or more forces. Although classifications can be somewhat arbitrary, most critics recognize four types of conflict (in no particular order).

The first involves one human being pitted against (opposed by) another—protagonist versus antagonist. If you've ever witnessed a boxing match, you've seen, firsthand, an example of this type of conflict. In a mystery novel, the conflict may be between detective and murderer. Or between murderer and intended victim. In a Romance (with a capital R), the conflict may be between a man and a woman (who, in the end, inevitably fall in love). Or it may involve the rivalry of two people for the affections of a third. The conflict in any play or novel or short story may be physical (on the battlefield, for example, or at the ballpark) or nonphysical (two people applying for the same job; two mathematicians vying to be the first to solve an enigma).

The second type of conflict pits man against nature. This can involve fierce storms or raging fires, or extreme cold or the heat of the desert, or voracious insects or venomous serpents—any inhospitable environment that threatens death or injury or serious illness.

The third type is inner conflict: the struggle within a person—mentally, emotionally, spiritually. This may be as simple a matter as Mary trying to make up her mind whether to go to the prom with John or with Bill; or Hamlet making up his mind to avenge his father's death; or Dr. Faust deciding whether to sell his soul to the devil.

The fourth type pits the protagonist against society. This can be as simple as flouting the dictates of the latest fashion, or defying the mores and morals of a community, or of a nation.

Most plays and novels, and most short stories as well, will contain more than one conflict, and usually more than one type of conflict. In the prologue to *Marmalade and Murder*, the initial conflict is inner: the little girl knows that it is unwise to venture off by herself, and onto ice despite her parents' prohibition, but does so anyhow. The primary conflict is man (female child) against nature—the struggle to save herself from drowning. There is also the threat of another conflict, between the child and the man who is running towards her.

Later, there is conflict between two friends. Cheryl, the younger woman, struggles against being led into precarious situations by the older Lena, who wants the two of them to play amateur detective. This conflict persists throughout the entire novel. Cheryl endures inner conflict—doubt, mistrust, and a host of other emotions—in her romantic relationship with one of the murder suspects; this, too, persists throughout.

Without giving away too much of the plot, I can only add that there are numerous episodes of conflict—struggle—between one or both of the women, on the one hand, and other characters of varying degrees of evil and criminality on the other. There are instances of conflict involving characters other than the two women. Some of these conflicts are relatively minor; others result in death. There's even a struggle against nature—a killer frost which endangers the cranberry crop.

A useful exercise might be to reread a favorite story, of whatever length, and pay close attention to the instances of conflict.

Point of View

From whose perspective is the action seen or narrated? Every work of fiction, whether literary or genre, requires a point of view: someone from whose perspective the story is told. That someone may be the god-like, all-knowing author (**omniscient**); or one of the characters—usually a main character, though not always—using the pronoun *I* (**first person**); or the author showing events through one or more of the characters, using *he* or *she* (**third person**).

First person is sometimes easiest to write, but has its limitations: everything has to be experienced by or thought by or told to the narrator. Things have to be described the way that person would experience them—within his or her limitations. This seeming disadvantage can actually be advantageous; skillful authors have told stories from the point of view of a young child, or a mentally retarded person, who does not understand the full meaning of events as they unfold. (This is also known as the **innocent eye**.) We, as mature readers, gradually understand important truths which the narrator, in his or her naiveté, does not. This—the naive first person point of view—works best for imparting irony, or perhaps for a certain kind of surprise ending. A close relative of the naive (innocent eye) narrator is the unreliable one—whom the reader cannot trust to tell the truth, or the whole truth. He or she may be lying, or merely biased (and not be aware of the bias), or deliberately distorting things by withholding information. This too, is a good way to achieve irony.

Most first person narrators, however, are neither naive nor unreliable, but rather, merely human—as naive or unreliable as the next guy, or less, or more so. They can be sympathetic, one with whom the reader readily identifies; or unsympathetic, one whom the reader instantly dislikes. Of course, an unsympathetic narrator can, for a variety of reasons, in the course of a novel or short story become sympathetic.

The first person point of view works best if you want to create a sense of intimacy, or immediacy, or perhaps authenticity ("I saw this happen with my own eyes"); or to establish a confessional, or a casual, tone. It allows you to be informal, even chatty. You can—in fact, you have to—adapt your style to the narrator. An uneducated laborer is not going to narrate a story the way a college professor would. A nineteen-year-old woman is going to present her story in a manner that is far different from her ninety-year-old grandmother's. If your first person narrator is radically different from you—in character, personality, intelligence, level of education, experience of the world; is the opposite sex, or much older or younger, or lived in the distant past, or resides on another planet, or is an animal or an intelligent robot—you've got your work cut out for you. If your narrator dies at the end of the story, how do you account for him or her telling it? Did he or she keep a diary? Is the person telling the story a ghost? Or do you, at some point, leave off, and introduce a different narrator—and another point of view?

Does the first person work for detective fiction? Most assuredly. Detectives themselves often make great narrators—especially in the Private Eye genre. The reader is privy to the thoughts of, and discovers clues along with, the detective. The reader may closely identify with, may even—for the duration of the book—*become*, the detective.

A minor character—one not directly involved in the action—can make an excellent first person narrator, someone who from a distance quietly observes, and comments upon, the events as they unfold. You can even, in a whodunit, have as your first person narrator the murderer—though I wouldn't advise it. Remember, you have to play fair with the reader. True, Agatha Christie managed it perfectly well. But then, how many Agatha Christies are there?

The omniscient point of view allows for far more freedom—sometimes too much. You can enter everyone's mind—including, in a mystery novel, that of the murderer. You can shift around from scene to scene, even from past to future and back again. You, the author / narrator, can intrude by directly commenting on the action. This may have worked fine for the Victorians, but doesn't necessarily work for us. Modern authors often choose the omniscient point of view, but keep their distance. They show events, enter into characters' minds, but refrain from commenting on the action, or directly addressing the reader.

I chose third-person limited for *Marmalade and Murder*: everything is seen and experienced through (limited to) one character—Cheryl Fernandes, the college professor who becomes a reluctant amateur detective at the urging of her newfound friend, the elderly Lena Lombardi. Limiting the third person to just one character allowed more freedom than the first person—I, the author, could wax poetic or be profound; best of all I could manipulate to create suspense. I could enter or leave this one character's mind at will. I could stand at a distance, or zoom up close, as it were.

There are far more variations for point of view—ways that authors can present their stories—than space allows for discussion. For example, the point of view character may be nothing more than a camera; we, the reader, see or otherwise perceive everything which he or she sees or perceives, but we never enter the character's mind; we have no idea what he or she is thinking, or feeling, or knows (about the past, for instance). There's the exact opposite, the **stream of consciousness**—the recording or depiction of the inner experiences of the mind. There are multiple (or shifting) points of view, there are—well, just too many to fit here.

The important thing (I almost said *point*) to remember is, whatever point of view you decide upon will determine, to a large extent, the type of story you write. More than one writer (myself included) has begun a short story or even a novel, only to realize halfway through that the point of view was all wrong. At that point (sorry!), you either scrap the whole project, and turn to something else, or you begin all over again.

An interesting exercise, for beginning or even experienced writers, might be to write a short story using one point of view, then rewrite that same story using another point of view. You might, for example, tell a love story using a first person narrator—a woman named Sally. She tells us, using the pronoun *I*, of a romantic encounter she had in Paris, and how it ended tragically. Once you've written the story in the first person, turn around and write it again. And again, write it from Sally's perspective—but use the third person limited point of view—the pronoun *she*. Even though you as author enter Sally's mind and record her thoughts (the same thoughts she had when *she* was the narrator) and relate the same events that she related, this second story will be far different from the first.

Memoirs: Stories Only You Can Tell

Now for a change of pace...

No matter what genre you're attempting, it's always a good idea to keep **pacing** in mind. Take nonfiction, for instance—a how-to book, on the subject of, say, writing, with a title that goes something like this, *Secrets and Shortcuts For Successful Writing...*, with a subtitle of, oh I don't know, let's say You *Can Learn from* My *Mistakes*.

Okay, I'm being a wise guy again. The point, however, is that pacing is important for many genres other than just mystery novels (where, admittedly, it is extremely important). It's something that you, the writer, have to be constantly aware of. In planning this book, one of the considerations was pacing—how the various chapters fit together, what should follow or precede what.

You, the reader, have been subjected to a number of consecutive chapters on the subject of writing mysteries, a genre with which you may have no more than a casual interest. True, as I've iterated (*ad nauseum*), the skills you learn for one genre are frequently applicable to others. Such is the case with pacing. But many of you are eager to move on to something else. Ghost stories would seem a logical choice with which to follow mysteries; the two genres have much in common. But no, you want a change of pace: hence memoirs—a genre in which, you guessed it, pacing while not the prime consideration is nonetheless a significant one.

❖

Memoirs. Memories. Recollections. Thinking back.

What is the hottest nonfiction genre today? Memoirs—becoming more popular, perhaps, than the novel.

Rock Village Publishing, the company my wife and I established in 1999, though small (scarcely fifty titles to date) has published a dozen or so memoirs. In fact, our first book was *Deep Meadow Bog*, my own memoirs of growing up on the cranberry bogs of southeastern Massachusetts in the 1950's. At the time of this writing, the summer of 2008, it is in its third printing, soon to go into a fourth.

Let me share a secret: I did not sit down to write a book of memoirs. I began by writing stories and essays, mostly vignettes, about my youth on the cranberry bogs. Over the years a number of these were published, in regional magazines, literary journals, and even in one or two anthologies. It wasn't until I had enough of these to fill the pages of a book that I decided to come out with *Deep Meadow Bog*.

One way to write a book is piecemeal. It's less painful that way, so long as you remain patient. In fact, I wrote my second book, *Shapes That Haunt New England*, a collection of ghost stories, in the same manner: one story at a time. These, too, saw publication over a span of years, in various journals, magazines, and anthologies. Naturally, I was writing them at the same time that I was writing the memoirs that would become *Deep Meadow Bog*, along with other things, such as poetry and humorous verse.

The way to write a book is one word, one sentence, one page at a time. And there's no law that says you can't work on more than one book at the same time.

❖

Deep Meadow Bog led to a second book of memoirs, *Cranberry Chronicles*. Readers who enjoyed the first book wanted to know what had become of many of the people depicted in it, so I obliged them with a sequel. It, too, has seen multiple printings.

You don't have to be famous to write your memoirs. Far from it. *Deep Meadow Bog* and *Cranberry Chronicles* filled a need; until they appeared, scarcely anything had been written about "life on the bogs." People—both locals and tourists—were curious about cranberry culture, and found the material very interesting, even fascinating.

You, too, can fill a need, or a niche—an area of interest that few, or none, have written about. That's exactly what Lena Britto did. You don't have to wait as long as she did, however; she was in her early eighties when she completed *Yankee Mericana*, which is part autobiography, part memoir. (The distinction between the two genres is a fine one, not important enough to go into here.)

Lena wrote about growing up in a small New England town, Rochester, Massachusetts, in the 1920's and '30's, and about her extraordinary life. She quit school when she was fifteen, graduated from college in her sixties, married and raised a family in the meantime, had a number of meaningful careers, and met and befriended many famous people while doing all this.

The niche she filled, however, besides authoring a book that would have been of great interest notwithstanding, was to write about the Cape Verdean experience—not only here, in New England, but in Cape Verde as well (where she was known as "Mericana"—The American). She visited the islands numerous times, and recorded her experiences and the people she met. I won't recount any more of her exploits here—read the book!—

but I will say that *Yankee Mericana* is the book that I, as a publisher and editor, am most proud of.

❖

Now, suppose that you do not have your own niche—a cozy little nook and cranny of the world that only you can write about—suppose your life has been an average one (if such a thing exists; aren't all lives, in their own way, extraordinary?), and that thousands, more likely millions, if not tens of millions, of people have lived lives similar to yours. Does that mean that your memoirs would be of little interest to readers?

No way, José.

Take Ann Liza Morse, for instance. At this very moment Rock Village Publishing is preparing Ann's fourth book of memoirs for publication. That's right: her fourth!

Admittedly, Ann's books are rather short. Even so, four volumes of memoirs is a significant achievement, especially when you consider that each book earns her more and more readers—readers who readily become eager to devour the previous entries in the series.

Did I say series?

Yes. Ann began with *Cranberry Kids*, followed by *Cranberry Kids on Cape Cod*, then *Cranberry Capers*, and finally (so far!) *Cranberry Kids: "Homecoming."* Titling the books as a series was a shrewd marketing ploy on Ann's part. Even with entirely different titles the books would have done well, but by making them more identifiable they've done even better. Readers who enjoyed *Cranberry Kids* (a category which surely includes everyone who has read it) would naturally gravitate toward a similarly titled book.

So is Ann filling a niche?

Not really. Despite the cranberry aspect of the titles,

cranberry bogs play only a minor role in her books. They're actually about growing up on a small farm in a small Cape Cod town (and moving to another Cape Cod town) in the 1930's, '40's, and '50's. What makes them so special is the way Ann captures the nostalgia, the humor, the whimsy, the quaintness of the era. She has a gift for writing succinctly—for the most part, each vignette is only a page or two in length—and for capturing the essence of everyday experience. She makes you, the reader, wish that you had grown up along with her, so that you could have shared with her the warmth, the joys, and yes the hardships, of those early years.

Take for instance the very first "story" in her first book, *Cranberry Kids*, titled "Electric Shocks." It's scarcely one page in length. But—and this is a point worth repeating over and over again—there is not one excess word, not a single syllable that could have been left out. She begins, "We lived in a two-story, A-roofed farmhouse with a kitchen ell and bathroom stuck on the very end. Since Mother had to heat hot water for the tub, we three girls bathed together. Edith had the deep end by the faucets. I was in the middle, and Barbie, the youngest, was stuck with the shallow end."

In that brief paragraph we learn what a lesser writer might have taken a whole page, or many pages, to say. Much of what she tells us is implied. In effect, Ann does what any good writer does: gives her readers credit for being able to figure things out for themselves; she knows that it is not necessary to state the obvious.

In her second, two-sentence, paragraph she gives us additional information about the rituals of bathing on a small farm; in the third paragraph she relates, almost casually, "Once a thunderstorm came up while we splashed around in the bathtub, and a bolt of lightning came so close to our house that we felt the electricity pass right through our bodies."

She then compares the shock she and her sisters felt to the shock they received from touching the electric fence that surrounded their fourteen-acre farm, and continues with "Visitors to our neighborhood, kids of all sizes, were quickly introduced to the mysteries of Morses' barnyard fence. A group of our neighborhood gang would line up holding hands, with the new kid on the far end. The first person in line grabbed hold of the fence—sending the electric shock through each kid and right back to the surprised visitor."

"Electric Shocks" sets the tone for the rest of the book: an old-fashioned New England childhood, filled with mischief and fond memories and lots of humor, and a little bit of *Tom Sawyer* to boot.

Regardless of your age, you can begin, today, to write your own memoirs. If you're ninety years old, rejoice—you've lived to a ripe old age and, no matter how "average" your life, you have experienced enough to fill an encyclopedia, if you will only take the time to muse and reflect. If, on the other hand, you're only ten years old, you can begin to jot down your daily experiences for use later, at a more mature age—fifteen, let's say. And if you're any age in between, you're in a position to reflect upon your past, and to share your joys and insights, pains and griefs with others.

Now, just because memoirs are nonfiction, there's no reason why you cannot apply some of the tricks of the trade we discussed earlier, in connection with mysteries and other works of fiction. We've already referred to pacing: you'll want to hook your reader (as Ann Morse did, with the childhood scene of herself and her two sisters crammed together in a tub and being nearly electrocuted). There's that tinge of alarm we feel, followed by the amusing account of the electric fence. Ann continues to hold our interest with the next vignette, about their cow Molly, who allowed the children to ride her, and who had a habit of showing up for Sunday School.

Wisely, though, Ann varies her narrative with accounts of her parents and other relatives, and with descriptions of what it was like living through the Great Depression and World War II. She knows when to alternate humor with more serious offerings. She occasionally uses dialogue to enliven the narrative.

In my own memoirs I made frequent use of the techniques of fiction. I submitted much of the earlier material to editors in the guise of short stories, as if they were fiction, and indeed several were published as such. And why not? I was doing what most writers of fiction do—drawing on my own experiences. The fact that the characters and events which I was depicting were real did not make the stories any the less interesting. I used a hook to capture the reader's attention and to hold it, and used devices such as dialogue to carry the story along.

I varied these "stories" with vignettes that were more of the essay type: more description, little or no dialogue, with the interest lying in details and background rather than in character development or plot. Although I did not portray events in precise chronological order—I skipped around a lot—I did build the material to a gradual climax, aging the "characters"—the people whom I'd known personally on the bogs—as I went along.

There's no one proper way to write memoirs. You can approach them in various ways. You can begin with the beginning of your life and work forward, with the end of your life and work backward, or somewhere in the middle. Or, if you're writing strict memoirs as opposed to autobiography, you can write about just one period or aspect of your life experience. You can depict, analyze, describe, lament, whatever. The one thing which you must do—as with all writing—is to apply all your knowledge and skills, to write and rewrite, keeping, always, the reader in mind.

Shocks and Shivers: Ghosts and Horror

Closely allied to the mystery, and yet worlds apart (make that *other* worlds), ghost stories are, with the possible exception of folktales and myths, perhaps the oldest genre—definitely the oldest, when you consider the frequency with which spirits and other apparitions occur in both folklore and mythology.

Let's look at the similarities between mysteries and ghost stories. (In the past, the two were often lumped together in bookstores and libraries. But that was before horror was recognized as a distinct category and given its own section. Nowadays you're likely to find collections of ghost stories resting—but not in peace!—on the shelves next to, or mingled in with, works of more explicit horror.) The very idea of ghosts is mysterious; what, exactly, are they? The spirits of dead people—visitants from an afterlife? Illusions? After-images that, like photographs, linger? Psychic phenomena? Wrinkles in time? Demons from hell sent to deceive mere mortals? The possibilities are endless.

Many traditional ghost tales, in their opening pages, are indistinguishable from detective stories. Something puzzling occurs—perhaps a baffling "mystery." There may even be unexplained deaths. What's going on?

And the atmosphere of the two genres is often similar.

"Atmosphere" in the mystery novel is desirable, though not essential. But in the ghost story it is paramount. Most ghost stories are intended to send cold shivers up and down the spine; to do so they quite often rely on spooky settings: dilapidated buildings, decaying mansions, graveyards at midnight, lonely fens. Many mysteries employ similar backgrounds.

Besides puzzling occurrences and sinister settings, the two genres often feature an element of danger; a character or group of characters may feel threatened—may indeed be in grave peril. M. R. James, the greatest ghost story writer of all times, insisted that the ghost in any ghost story must be malevolent—must have evil intentions, or at least pose a threat. People, including innocent people, sometimes die as a result of the hauntings; ghost stories frequently have "unhappy" endings. In this latter respect they are different from mysteries, in which a happy ending, if not absolutely essential, is at least expected. There are degrees of "happiness," of course; but as we saw in an earlier chapter, at the end of the traditional mystery novel the sense of order in society, which has been seriously disrupted, is restored—the surviving characters pick up the pieces, as it were, and resume their lives.

In the ghost story the opposite is often the case: the sense of order—of what is real and unreal—may be terribly askew. Ordinary laws of nature no longer apply; life is unsettled; two plus two no longer equals four.

The primary difference—and it's a big one—between the two types of stories is that the mystery in a mystery novel must not involve the supernatural. It's all right to have events appear to be ghostly in nature; it's even okay to have a real ghost, in a minor role, lurking here or there in the background— so long as the solution to the mystery, the explanation of the crime or crimes, depends only on what we normally think of as natural phenomena.

❖

So, if pure mystery novels must *not* make use, other than tangentially, of the supernatural, does it follow that all ghost stories *must* involve it? The answer to this question, one would think, is, why yes, of course. Doesn't common sense tell you that if it's called a ghost story, it must contain a ghost? Gimme a break! Even a four-year-old child could figure that one out.

Most four-year-olds, however, do not write ghost stories. And that's probably a good thing. For a ghost story does not necessarily have to be about ghosts, or even contain elements of the supernatural. Admittedly, there should be at least a hint of the uncanny, or of the weird—an intimation that all in our lives is not what it seems. Lacking that, there should be some sort of "unusual" element, such as a strange quirk of fate: *something* beyond the ordinary—whatever that is!

If ghost stories are frequently categorized as horror, are the two one and the same?

Yes and no. Although some folks (scholars, academics, critics, ordinary readers, or what have you) refer to ghost stories as horror, others reserve the designation *horror* for stories which involve the physical, rather than the supernatural: tales of unspeakable tortures or other unpleasant fates: being entombed alive, let us say, or slowly eaten by insects, or buried up to the neck in sand as the tide slowly comes in, or perhaps merely spending a lifetime in an unlit dungeon for a crime one didn't commit—that sort of thing. Another name for this type of story, borrowing from the French, is *conte cruel*.

There are those who prefer the term *weird fiction* to ghost story. Others opt for *tales of the uncanny* or *macabre*. An older term, somewhat outdated, refers to *off-trail* stories. And many, if not most, of those die-hards who insist on the term *ghost story* would include, as honorary ghosts I suppose, such entities as vampires, ghouls, witches, werewolves, and other "children of the night."

❖

Whatever name we decide to call them, the stories we've been discussing in this chapter all fall into the broader category of fiction—both literary fiction and so-called genre fiction. It's important to keep in mind that many of our greatest authors wrote, among other things, ghost stories: Charles Dickens, for instance; Henry James; Edith Wharton; Elizabeth Bowen; even Mark Twain.

I mention this because of an unfortunate tendency these days for some readers to dismiss fiction as being somehow unworthy. I ran into this tendency when I published my first book of ghost stories, *Shapes That Haunt New England.* At signings people would frequently ask, "Are these stories true?" When I told them no, they're fiction, many lost interest, saying "I want to read stories that are *true*." It would be fruitless no doubt to point out to these naive folks that good fiction strives for, and frequently attains, a much higher *truth* than mere nonfiction.

In any case, fictional ghost stories are an entirely different animal from "true" ghost stories. Both types have a place in our literature. Although I've written dozens of both fictional and nonfictional ghost stories, however, I'll restrict my comments on the latter to a handful of sentences.

The fascination with true ghost stories, it seems, stems from the fact, or supposition, that such things can be. My own interest in the genre has two sources—a lifelong interest in folklore, in the legends, fairy tales, beliefs, superstitions, and traditions of unsophisticated, often unlettered, people; and in self-defense as a writer and speaker, so that when asked, "Are these stories true?" I could honestly reply, "Why yes, of course."

Being an enterprising fellow, I learned to embellish the true ghost stories I came upon—either in my research through obscure books, or from chatting with folks who came to me at signings or after talks to share their personal experiences of the paranormal—I learned to embellish these true stories with elements of fiction. Now, that does not necessarily mean that I "made things up." It does mean that I used elements of fictional writing—hooks, pacing, development of characters, atmosphere, dialogue—to make the stories even more interesting than they would be if merely "reported."

Some true ghost stories—weird happenings that cannot be explained without resorting to the supernatural—are so fascinating in and of themselves that they are best told in a straightforward manner, as if in a story for a newspaper or an article for a magazine. Such stories may involve a sequence of events that constitute a plot of sorts. These stories do not require embellishment, but rather, your carefully crafted, well-thought-out sentences, leaving your reportage of the facts to create its proper sense of awe (or wonderment, or abject terror).

If you love ghost stories and wish to write your own, my best advice is to reread your favorite tales, whether they be by Edgar Allan Poe, E. F. Benson, Marjory Lawrence, or any one of the many hundreds of other fine writers of the macabre who have enriched English literature over the past two (or even three) hundred years. Study them. What makes them so interesting? The suspense, to be sure—the shudders they induce, the delicious fear of the dark, of being alone at night in an old house. But how was that suspense created? Don't imitate your favorite authors—not outright. But do learn from them. Apply some of the tricks you've acquired from reading this book (comparing them to the techniques used by the authors of the ghost stories you're reading).

One trick, old as the hills but still effective, is to build up the "ghost"—the haunting—gradually, bit by bit. Don't try to shock your reader—not right away; save that for the ending. Introduce the ghost by merely hinting at something amiss; then slowly increase the pressure. One way to do this is by *not* allowing the reader to "see" the ghost—again, not right away, and perhaps not at all.

Put your readers' imaginations to work for you. The horrors which you hint at but do not fully explain will be far more terrifying to the reader than any that you attempt to depict in detail.

One final word of advice: clichés. Avoid them. For example (and I'll limit the examples to only one) blood-sucking vampires in the form of bats are pretty worn out by now. Try something new, or at least an original twist on something old. But that, of course, is something you should do no matter what type of fiction, nonfiction, play, or poetry you are creating.

The Nitty Gritty of Writing Dialogue

One evening recently at a local library, during a question-and-answer session, an aspiring young writer raised her hand from the audience and asked: "How do you handle dialogue?"

The guest speaker, a noted author, pretended to misunderstand the question. As if deep in thought he tugged at his beard, and with a twinkle in his eye replied: "How do *I* handle dialogue?" He paused. "In the usual way, I guess." One or two members of the audience chuckled at the witticism; the others, perhaps out of sympathy for the young woman, refrained from laughter.

Undaunted, she politely rephrased her question: "How do you—how does anyone—deal with the problem of dialogue? I guess what I mean is, what are the secrets to making characters in a story seem believable—making them sound like real people when they talk to one another? It seems that when I try to write dialogue it comes off sounding stilted—unnatural."

"Dialogue can be a problem," the author agreed. "The best advice I can give is, develop an ear for it. Read widely. Pay attention to how other writers handle it."

Apparently not satisfied by the answer to her question, the aspiring young writer frowned, and was about to raise her hand again when someone else, an older member of the audience, piped up. "Aw, com'on," he urged the author. "Lighten up. Tell us your secrets."

"I have no secrets," the author insisted. Then, appearing to relent, he added: "Well, perhaps one or two. Look," he said, "I was serious when I advised you to read widely. Frankly, that's the best way—the only way—to develop a keen ear for dialogue. When you do write your own dialogue, read it aloud to yourself, to hear how it actually sounds. In fact, if you're a beginning writer—or even a more experienced one—it's not a bad idea to read aloud everything you write, so that you can pick up on any awkward phrases."

"Do you read your own stuff aloud to yourself?" someone asked.

"No. I guess probably because I've read so many thousands of books in my lifetime, and because I began to read at such a very early age, I developed an ear early on."

"What's this 'ear' you keep talking about?" an elderly woman demanded.

"The term is borrowed from the field of music. I don't know of any other way to express it, except to say that you develop a sensitivity to the rhythms of speech, to the way people actually talk."

"But," the aspiring young writer asked, "wouldn't it make better sense to listen carefully to conversations around you—without eavesdropping of course—and even record the exact phrasing that people use? Why would you want to 'develop an ear' by reading when you have the real thing around you all the time?"

Several audience members nodded in agreement. "Now *that* makes sense," one of them said.

The distinguished author shook his head. "I'm afraid that it does *not* make sense."

A handful of people in the audience eyed him skeptically. Several others appeared to squirm uncomfortably in their seats. *The man is dancing mad*, they seemed to be thinking. *He has been bitten by the tarantula.*

"Do you mean to tell us," asked a young man who up to now had remained quietly seated, "that carefully recording how people in real life actually converse with one another is not the best way to learn how to write believable dialogue?"

"I mean to say exactly that," the noted speaker replied. He allowed time for his words to sink in before continuing. "In fact, there are not one, but two, very good reasons for not attempting to duplicate on the page the actual speech that you hear around you.

"The first is, that people in real life do not speak smoothly. They pause, they stammer, they interrupt themselves and one another. They start a sentence and fail to finish it. They start speaking about one thing and end up talking about something else entirely. They repeat themselves. They mispronounce words. They make grammatical errors. They hem and they haw. Over and over again, they use annoying phrases such as 'you know' or 'like I say.' If you were to duplicate or imitate this on the page you'd have complete chaos. Your readers would lose patience trying to follow your dialogue; you'd infuriate them."

"But," the formerly silent young man protested, "suppose the character you're portraying is that sort of person—a poor speaker. You might even want to emphasize in your story the fact that he lacks speaking skills. You wouldn't want him to talk like a college professor, now would you?"

"Of course not. But a point always to keep in mind when writing dialogue is that a little goes a long way. You might have your poor speaker repeat himself once, or commit one or two grammatical errors, or clear his throat now and then. Your readers will readily get the point, without your shoveling it down their throats. The same principle, incidentally, holds true when writing dialect, or portraying someone who speaks English with a heavy foreign accent. F'r instance, suh, s'posin' yore leadin' lady is a li'l' ol' Suthin' gel from th' state a' Miss'ssipi. Yu'all kin convey that fact with just one or two instances of her distinct verbal mannerisms. By all means sprinkle those mannerisms throughout her dialogue, but sparingly."

"You almost have to develop an instinct for what your readers will tolerate," the aspiring young woman said.

"That's another way of putting it," the speaker agreed. He took a sip of water from a plastic bottle and stood facing the audience, as if waiting for the next question.

"You said there was a second reason for not imitating real speech," the young man reminded him.

"That's right, I did," the speaker said, nodding his thanks. "The second reason is even more important than the first. And that reason is, the spoken language and the written language are not one and the same thing. In fact, they're two different things entirely. The written language is only a close approximation of the spoken language."

At this point the elderly woman, who had been maintaining a stony silence as if feeling rather put out by the proceedings, spoke up. "You're not making sense. In one breath you tell us to read the written works of others in order to develop this thing called 'ear,' and in the next breath you tell us that the spoken language, the sense of which we want to convey in our own writing, is not the same thing as the written language. So why read the written in order to convey the spoken?"

"You read the written because you write the written," the noted author stated, rather wearily it seemed. He looked at the bottle of water on the table next to him as if wishing it were something a bit stronger. "Getting back to the differences between the written and spoken languages: when we speak, we not only say words—vowels and consonants—we inflect them.

We stress syllables. We raise or lower our voices. We speak slowly, or rapidly. Moreover, we gesture, we gesticulate, with our hands. We convey meanings by intonations, by facial expressions, by rolling our eyes, by moving our heads. We point. For emphasis some folks—no one in this audience, I trust—spit. We laugh, we sigh, we chuckle, we sob. Our colors change; we blanch with fear or pain, turn red with anger or embarrassment. The printed word conveys but a fraction of all this."

"So," the aspiring young writer, with a bright smile on her face, said, "*that's* why we can't just record what we hear. We also have to convey all the subtleties. I can see, as an aspiring young writer, that I've got my work cut out for me."

A middle-aged woman, seated in the back row, raised her hand. "Can I ask a question?"

"By all means," the speaker said, rolling his eyes, as if to say, *Have I refused anyone yet?* Or perhaps the meaning he wished to convey was, *Do I have a choice?*

"This is probably a trivial question, but, do you have any pointers on the use of the word *said?* You know, when to write 'he said' or 'they said'—that sort of thing. Or should we vary *said* with *stated* or *asseverate*d or *declared* or…"

"Yes," the guest speaker interrupted, "the possibilities are endless, aren't they. The best rule of thumb is to stick with *said* for statements and *asked* (rather than, say, *queried* or *interrogated*) for questions. *Said* and *asked* become nearly invisible; variations call attention to themselves. Certainly, though, when appropriate, use something stronger, such as *insisted* or *exclaimed* or *muttered.* Unless you're writing humor, or fantasy involving talking dogs, avoid absurdities such as 'Get out of my way,' he *barked* or 'Wow, that's some good looking dame,' he *whistled.* Of course, you can omit the phrase entirely."

"You mean, like this?"

"Exactly."

"But won't that confuse the reader as to who is speaking?"

"Not necessarily. Especially not if you're careful to make each character sound like a distinct individual."

"How is that done?"

"Each of us speaks in a way that reveals certain things about ourselves: our level of education, the region of the country (or world) we're from, what sort of work we do, the types of books we read, or whether we read books at all. A coarse person uses coarse language. A childish person uses childish language—the diction and grammar and other things that make up our speech. Our personalities and perceptions of the world vary; it's your job as a writer to capture all that on paper. Or electronically. I keep forgetting we live in the Age of the Computer."

The speaker paused to take a final swig from the water bottle. At that point the Director of the library rose from her seat in the last row and approached the podium. "Thank you, Mr. Lodi," she said, with a gracious smile. "I'm afraid our time for this part of the program is up. But on behalf of everyone here tonight I want to extend our appreciation for such an informative talk." Turning to the audience, she announced: "Refreshments are being served in the next room. We've also set up a table where Mr. Lodi will be signing copies of his book—this book, I believe, the one that contains this chapter that we're all in. He'll be happy to answer any further questions, I'm sure, for each of you personally. Won't you, Mr. Lodi?"

"Of course," he replied with a smile. "Though any answers I give from this point on will be off the record. This is the end of the chapter on dialogue."

Poetry Versus Verse

Although the two terms are often used interchangeably, there's a vast difference between poetry and verse. Artistically, poetry is the loftier form, verse the more humble. Both, of course, are difficult to write; to say that verse is the lesser form is not to dismiss it lightly. (For those who are paying attention, that last sentence was a feeble attempt at wordplay—Light Verse being a highly respected genre.)

This is probably as good a place as any for placement of the fine print: i.e., the disclosure of my credentials—or lack of them—for writing this chapter. By no means do I consider myself a serious poet. I know personally, and have published books by, a number of fine poets; I do not pretend to classify myself with them. That said, I have published poetry and light verse in dozens of magazines and journals—*Ellery Queen's Mystery Magazine*, for example, and the prestigious *Light—A Quarterly of Light Verse*. Several of my poems were selected by a New York outfit for use in software designed for adult education. (They actually paid well for the right to use the poems—which, strictly speaking, are not poems at all but, rather, light verse). And the editor of a respected poetry journal selected me as "Poet-of-the-Quarter." She even nominated me for a Pushcart Prize. I didn't win, but it was a great honor just to have been nominated.

In college and graduate school I studied poetry along with many other subjects relevant to language and literature. I have taught English Literature, including poetry, at the college level. The study and teaching of poetry, by themselves, do not make one a poet. But it's a safe bet that, unless you are an original genius of, say, the Shakespeare caliber, you cannot write worthwhile poetry without having some familiarity with what has been written before, as well as what is currently being written. And even Shakespeare, that sly dog, genius that he was, was extremely well read. For example, he lifted the plots for many of his plays from other sources. (But wasn't it T. S. Eliot who said, "Good writers borrow; great writers steal.")

I mention all this for no other purpose than to justify my right to pontificate on the subject of poetry. As an editor, I have received hundreds of manuscripts, many of them collections of poems—or what purported to be poems. Sadly—and not unexpectedly—most of it was atrocious stuff. Is it cruel and heartless of me to dismiss it as such? Perhaps—but consider my doing so an expression of "tough love."

I have in my library two collections of "poetry" so bad that it is fun to read: *The Stuffed Owl: An Anthology of Bad Verse*; and *Pegasus Descending: A Treasury of the Best Bad Poems in English*. (These are collections, mind you, of poems which their authors wrote with serious intent; their purpose was not to create laughter.) So much bad verse has been written (and, alas, published) that there is scarcely any duplication in the two books. Doubtless, sufficient material exists to supply many more such volumes.

Far too much of the so-called poetry I look at as an editor can be classified as **doggerel** (a word which derives, ultimately, from the word *dog*): loose, rhyming verse so badly written that it is embarrassing, even comical. None of it, however, was good enough (that is to say, bad enough) to merit inclusion in an anthology of junk poetry. Poetry has to be really, really bad to be comically good.

Am I, with my harsh assessment, discouraging any would-be poets?

I hope so. For if you are a true poet you will not be daunted, or adversely influenced, by anything which I have to say. You already have a love—a passion— for words, and for poetry, for reading, and for looking into the heart of things. You will, regardless of any gems of wisdom, or pseudo wisdom, attempted by me, persist and persevere. You will write, and rewrite, and see your best work rejected by fools. Undeterred, you will continue to write, and rewrite, and one day you will succeed and be acclaimed (by a mere handful, of course, because there are far more people writing poetry these days than reading it) as an accomplished poet, worthy of publication.

These words are not aimed at you, the true poet; rather, they are intended for any poetasters who may be perusing the pages of this book.

What, pray tell, is a poetaster?

Why, a **poetaster** is an inferior poet, one who writes poems of little or no worth.

What then, O sage, is poetry?

Is that snickering that I hear in the background? If so, it is not misplaced. The person who snickers—the snickerer— knows full well that there is no satisfactory definition of poetry. The snickerer knows, full well, that—when it comes to defining poetry—I, The Great Pontificator, am stumped. I cannot give a definition for that for which there is no definition—no satisfactory definition.

How does my favorite dictionary, *The American Heritage Dictionary of the English Language* (the 1969, 1970 edition), define poetry? Well, it starts off with "1. The art or work of a poet." Hmm—now that's a big help! Space—not to mention the patience of the reader—does not allow me to give the additional meanings; take my word for it: it doesn't get any better.

Now, *The American Heritage Dictionary* does give a somewhat better definition for **poem**—a definition that, if quoted here, would take up half a page—and require several chapters to explicate. I'll just give the beginning: "A composition designed to convey a vivid and imaginative sense of experience..." But isn't that what all creative writing attempts to do?

So, having beat around the bush, WHAT IS POETRY? Duh?

There resides on the shelves of my library—and has resided there these many decades, since I was an undergraduate at Boston University—an excellent reference work by a trio of esteemed editors titled *A Dictionary of Literary Terms* (published in 1960). The entry for **poetry** reads, in its entirety: "See *literature, versification, figurative language*, and the separate types, such as *elegy, lyric, ode.*"

Talk about evasive action!

Let's try another excellent reference—also titled *A Dictionary of Literary Terms* (this one published seventeen years later, in 1977). It contains a rather lengthy entry for **poem**. The word derives, we are told, from a Greek word meaning "something made, created." So far, so good. "Thus," our editor continues, "a work of art."

Huh? Now that really narrows it!

He goes on: "A metrical composition, a work of verse, which may be in rhyme (q.v.) or may be blank verse (q.v) or a combination of the two." Oh? What about free verse? Most poetry written in the last one hundred years has lacked rhyme, and is decidedly not blank verse.

Eventually we get to the truth: "In the final analysis what makes a poem different from any other kind of composition is a species of magic..."

Magic? Don't you just love it! Wait, it gets better: "...the secret to which lies in the way the words lean upon each other, are linked and interlocked in sense and rhythm, and thus elicit from each other's syllables a kind of tune whose beat and melody varies subtly and which is different from that of prose (q.v.)—'the other harmony.'"

Oh, now I get it—a poem is like a prison, and words are like prisoners, interlocked and linked (chained) together, leaning upon one another for support. No? Then whatever does he mean?

It's as clear as mud.

Perhaps the entry for **poetry** in the same book will illuminate the matter: "It is a comprehensive term which can be taken to cover any kind of metrical composition. However, it is usually employed with reservations, and often in contra-distinction to verse."

Enough!

In all fairness, the editors of both books do an excellent job of defining various terms, and give well-chosen examples to illustrate the definitions. The problem is, there's no satisfactory definition for poetry. You can describe it, talk about it, give examples of it. But you cannot pin it down. Poetry, it has been said, is like pornography—you cannot adequately define it, but you know it when you see it.

My advice to the budding poet: Read all the poetry you can get your grubby (or neat and petite) hands on. Read poetry that was written in the late Middle Ages, and that is being written in the present, and anything in between. Attend poetry readings. Talk to poets—for the most part they're lonely folks and will welcome the attention. Most of all, write poems and submit them to literary journals, and see what happens.

❖

Before moving on to light verse, I'll conclude this section with two poems of my own—both of which have been previously published—and one or two (more, actually) brief observations regarding them. Only you, the reader, can judge whether the poems are worthy of consideration—whether their author is a poet, or merely a poetaster. The first is one of three poems for which Cynthia Brackett-Vincent, editor of *The Aurorean*, nominated me for a Pushcart Prize.

The Clam Digger

Gulls gather like pigeons in a park
as the old man stoops and, gently,
sinks steel prongs into soft sand
and rips the belly of the beach in two.

He guts the shore as if it were a fish,
slicing clean, exposing soft-shelled clams
like pearls, like bits of flesh flensed
from the body of the sea.

Noisily the gulls squabble for the right
to forage in the rubble of his labor:
smashed shells, a worm or two, and clams
legally too small, though not for them.

The old man quickly fills his wire mesh bucket
then dips it in the surf to rinse.
A gull swoops to pluck away the topmost clam;
the old man shakes his fist, and laughs.

Let's take a quick look at the poem—not word by word, which is the way poetry should be analyzed (for lack of a better term), nor even line by line; doing so would take up too much space—but let's examine some of the elements (again, for lack of a better term) which we should look for when reading poetry (and when writing it!).

First, notice that not a word is wasted; that is, there are no words which could have been left out. When writing poetry, less is more. *And the same is true for prose.*

Whether writing fiction, nonfiction, poetry, or letters to the editor, be succinct; pare off all unnecessary words—a category which includes most adverbs. The next time you sit down to write something—a short story, the first chapter of that novel you've been mulling over, the love letter you've been meaning to send, a letter of complaint to the manufacturer of a shabby product, an entry in your diary or journal (which, having learned from my mistakes, you are of course keeping faithfully), a poem, whatever—give yourself a goal. Slash it by ten percent. Great! See how easy (or difficult) it is? But don't stop there. Slash it again. And again.

Okay, you can put the knife away—for now. (After you've let the work sit for a while—the longer the better—you can return to it and cut away some more. But for now you can let it lie there, bleeding.) Your next task is to examine each word, or group of words, and see whether you can substitute it or them with something better.

What's that? Oh, you thought we were examining my poem? Well, we are, but we got sidetracked. But okay, we can return to the poem and look at it closely. Look at the verbs especially. Is each the best choice for the sense of the poem? I think so. Could I have substituted something better for any one of them? I don't think I could have. (Remember, you're learning from my mistakes; if you could see the first draft of the poem—which I mercifully didn't keep—you'd see something entirely different; you'd probably see too many words, and weaker verbs, and any number of embarrassing lapses. But you're not seeing them, because I wrote; and rewrote, and—you guessed it! rewrote again.)

To summarize: you can achieve succinctness by eliminating all unnecessary words, and by choosing the right word (to replace a group of words). In writing prose, you can get away with a few extra words here and there. (This book, for example—I could make it more succinct, but in doing so I would lose some of the informality, the breeziness, the sense of chattiness, which I've striven to achieve. Just what and how much you cut depends on the style you are aiming for.) But in poetry, even one unnecessary word can be deadly—can ruin the whole poem.

Let's move on to another subject: figurative language.

(Almost all poetry makes use of figurative language—things like metaphors and similes. But then, so does prose. You can see, now, can't you, why poetry is so nearly impossible to define. Why, it's just like prose. But different.)

"Gulls gather like pigeons in a park"—why, that's a simile; that is to say, a metaphor.

Simile: a comparison of two dissimilar things, using *like* or *as*. (Gulls are like pigeons, in that, besides being birds, they form a loose, disordered, temporary group.)

Metaphor: 1. [in the narrower sense] an implied comparison; 2. [in the wider sense] figurative language in general, including simile.

"The old man...rips the belly of the beach in two"—why, that's a metaphor [in the narrower sense]. The comparison (of the beach like a living thing, having a belly) is implied.

"He guts the shore as if it were a fish" continues the metaphor, of the beach as a living thing. The reference to flensed flesh extends the metaphor even further. The point I wish to emphasize here is that figurative (metaphorical) language should be striking, as original as possible (without being outlandishly so), and consistent (the beach has a body, the sea has a body, etc.).

"Sinks steel prongs into soft sand" is an example of another poetical device (also useful with prose)—alliteration.

Alliteration: the repetition of initial sounds (at the beginnings of words or syllables).

In this case, initial *s* is repeated. (The ending *s*, on sinks and prongs, adds to the effect.) "*G*ulls *g*ather" is another example of alliteration, "*b*elly of the *b*each" still another.

We could go on, and talk about rhythm, and meter, but this book is too general for that. Read the poem out loud—you'll begin to sense, and feel, the rhythms and the meter. You'll hear echoes—of meanings as well as sounds—and you'll begin to appreciate, perhaps (if you don't already) the importance of applying the techniques of poetry to prose.

A second poem of mine follows. I won't take it apart, bit by bit; I include it merely to share with you the exuberance, the sense of liberation, it conveys: the sense of the joy of writing, of creating, of shaping things with words.

Reaching

Scoff if you will,
I have reached high
and touched the sky

have
felt with fingers ethereal

the silken softness of the blue

have
stroked the underbellies of billowing clouds

have
shaken hands with that old gent
God
that jolly giant of a deity

who
when I told him, "I'm a poet,"
laughed and said, "Awwwright!"

As a topic of discussion, light verse is somewhat easier to approach than poetry. "Playful poetry" is as good a description (notice I avoided the word *definition*!) as any. Whereas most modern poets eschew rhyme, using it sparingly if at all, writers of light verse depend on rhyme more than on any other poetic device.

Let's begin with a clarification. Most light verse—though not all—is intended to be humorous, or at least witty. It may, or may not, be satirical. Sometimes it is merely occasional—meaning that it celebrates, marks, or observes an occasion, whether it be someone's birthday, a holiday, a significant event, or the anniversary of a significant event. (Not all occasional poetry is light verse. A poem about a tragic event might be very serious—very heavy—indeed.)

Before looking at a few examples of light verse, let's talk about rhyme. In the popular mind, the word *poetry* conjures up *rhyme*. I have no idea what children study these days in school;

I assume at some point they are exposed to poetry of some kind. Those of us who belong to past generations were taught, and required to memorize, poems that rhymed (Longfellow comes to mind, and any number of other classic American and British poets). Rhyme is an important element of poetry because it aids memory. In times past, before the invention of writing, and even later, when the vast majority of any given population were illiterate, stories were passed on orally, often in the form of poems.

Ironically, rhyme is currently so much in disfavor that many literary journals specify in their guidelines, "no rhymed poetry." Why is this so?

For one thing, good poetry should sound original, fresh. And it's nearly impossible to come up with rhymes that haven't been used before—hundreds of times. Just how often can you rhyme *June* with *moon* and expect to get away with it? So, for the most part, rhyme is considered tired, outmoded. Someone like Ogden Nash could continually come up with original rhymes—but they sounded funny, which is exactly what he intended.

Another reason for rhyme being very much in disfavor is the way poetasters (would-be poets), in the mistaken belief that a poem is not a poem unless it rhymes, force it. "On this heart of mine / The sun did shine." Fine! But that last line is archaic; it's no longer the way we express the simple past tense. We say, instead, "The sun shone."

Well, I don't wish to belabor the obvious. But I do wish to emphasize that poetry, serious or light, should flow naturally. Should, that is, sound like everyday speech. Oh by no means all poetry—but certainly the poetry that anyone bothering to read this book is likely to attempt. Accomplished poets can write anything they choose; but they are not the ones for whom these words are intended.

What Every Gardener Knows

Among my gardening woes
(besides a stuffed-up nose)
I number: blistered toes,
a blight-afflicted rose,
a host of insect foes,
a leaking plastic hose
with nozzle that won't close,
seeds an ill wind blows,
thieving flocks of crows,
marauding bucks and does,
and neatly tended rows
where *nothing* ever grows.

❖

Now there's a poem with lines that rhyme—with a vengeance. Twelve lines, and all ending with the same sound. Wait—there's more; even the title rhymes. All, I trust, to humorous effect.

What else makes the poem work? (It originally appeared in *Light: A Quarterly of Light Verse* and was one of three poems selected by a New York firm for use in educational software; I later included it in my collection of light verse, *Ida, the Gift-Wrapping Clydesdale*. Incidentally, the idea for the Ida poem came to me in a dream. As Fats Waller was fond of saying, "One never knows, do one!")

First of all, it's true—as will agree, I'm sure, anyone who has attempted to create a garden. Allergies, weather, faulty equipment, animal pests—they're all there, presented at a rapid pace. The lines are short, so that anyone reading it, especially aloud, feels faintly out of breath—as if from frustration and exasperation.

And it ends with a not so subtle irony: neatly tended rows, implying arduous labor despite many setbacks—and all to no avail.

"What Every Gardener Knows" is a gardener laughing at his own folly—something with which most readers can identify, even if they've never gardened themselves.

I'll end this chapter with one more instance of light verse. Although it uses rhyme, the stanzas are not regular, so that while it is primarily an example of traditional verse, it does share some characteristics with free verse. (Once you know the rules, and can write traditional works, you will have earned the right to break those rules.)

Ella, the Flirtatious Clydesdale

Ella, while chomping on hay,
recalls that it's Valentine's Day.
Winking her eyes,
she smiles at the guys—
the sorrel, the roan, and the gray.

"I've always been fond of kissing,"
says Ella, reminiscing.

"I've had a mustang or two.
Been married to more than a few.

But now I'm single. I need
the love of a dashing steed.

"Is there a bronco, short or tall,
eager to share my stall?

"When I was a demoiselle,
I was spunky and full of hell.
If I let down my mane
it was never in vain—
I would kiss, but never tell!

"I was a frolicsome filly!
I wore hats both stylish and frilly.
With my permed-up hair
and flirtatious stare
I drove the young colts silly."

So stallions all, beware—
to tell the truth
she's long in the tooth—
but ever the madcap mare!

Appendix: Helpful & Humorous Tidbits

This appendix comprises a small selection of the dozens of vignettes about grammatical and other matters pertinent to the craft of writing which I wrote many years ago and published in various journals, magazines, and newspapers. At one time it was my intention to gather them together into a book; for one reason or another I never did so. The handful of monographs included here are representative; it is hoped they will prove of some value to the aspiring writer. (They start off with what would have been the Foreword to the book.)

Foreword

"If you're so smart," so goes the saying, "why ain't you rich?"

In other words what makes me—a humble juggler of vowels and consonants (*juggler*, from Latin *joculator*, meaning jester or trickster)— what makes *me* an expert on proper English usage?

"A passion for words, a lifelong love affair with the language," is the best answer I can provide. Certainly a graduate degree from Boston University and a number of years spent teaching English composition and literature to college freshmen have also contributed to my "expertise." Basically, though, I'm just a fellow who loves to read and write, who loves the feel and taste and shapes of words. And who has learned, ploddingly and painfully, from his own—often embarrassing—mistakes.

Many of the writing tips included in this slender volume are, in fact, direct results of my own verbal blunders and uncertainties. Did I at one time write "plain sailing?" Shouldn't it have been "*plane* sailing?" Composing a brief monograph on the subject helps cement it in my mind so that I don't make the same mistake twice.

And provides a resource for future reference (as in the following anecdote):

There once was a respected admiral in the Navy who had the habit every day of consulting a slip of paper which he kept locked in the top drawer of his desk. What nugget of wisdom was it, everyone who observed him wondered, that he so treasured? After a distinguished career that lasted many years the admiral finally retired. While rummaging through the desk one of his former subordinates came upon the slip of paper. When she unfolded it she saw the words, printed in neat block letters: "PORT *LEFT*, STARBOARD *RIGHT*."

Like the venerable admiral I have my own aids to memory, my own little slips of paper, which I consult more frequently than I care to admit. This little book contains a number of them.

While on the subject of mistakes, I'd like to take this opportunity to include the usual disclaimer: any howlers (such as misspellings, erroneous attributions, etc.) contained in this book are intentional and have been included solely to test the reader's acumen and intelligence. Or they have resulted from somebody else's carelessness or ignorance, not mine. Well, perhaps one or two—a dozen at most—can be attributed to me.

Except for the brief paragraphs relating to the word *dessert* (derived from a French word meaning "to clear the table") which fittingly occupy the last position, the material in this book is organized—or to forestall any adverse criticism, *dis*organized—with no particular pattern in mind. I conceived the book especially for writers and students of English, not as a reference but rather as a collection of epigrams or pensées suitable for casual or occasional reading and—if I have succeeded—rereading.

Oh, and *Caveat lector*: I'm a shameless punster.

Even so, I pun for only the right reasons: to emphasize a point, or as an aid to memory, or for the sheer fun of it.

Fun. That's the primary purpose of this book. To see the humor in words, to take the tedium out of the art of precise writing.

Though not a pedant (who, me?) I confess to being a grammarian of the old school: my penchant is for the prescriptive rather than the descriptive. I believe that if it ain't broke, don't fix it. *Disinterested* for example means one thing, *uninterested* something entirely different. This difference has served the language well these many years. I cannot agree with those who would assert that since *disinterested* is frequently used by careless writers to mean *uninterested*, grammarians should accept this new usage as inevitable.

Nor do I accept the use of *gender* when *sex* is meant. Admittedly, this latter objection—in these days of political correctness—is a battle already lost. I include a little essay on the subject ("Return to Gender, Sex Unknown") partly out of stubbornness, but also for the benefit of those who, setting their works of fiction in historical times, wish to avoid anachronisms by saying it accurately—like it was, baby!

At the beginning of this foreword I mentioned "proper English usage." For *proper* or *correct* you may substitute *traditional* or *standard*. Certain usages or locutions are universally accepted; others are not. Like body odor or bad breath, solecisms call attention to themselves. And like lapses in personal hygiene, verbal gaffes can lead to failing grades or that bugaboo of all writers: rejection.

Let Sleeping Verbs Lie

[This is the first of the many humorous pieces which I wrote to clarify (at first for myself, and eventually for others) points of grammar which I found sticky or bothersome. At this late date "Let Sleeping Verbs Lie" doesn't seem all that clever; it's rather obvious, if not downright lame. But getting it published encouraged me to think about other topics in need of clarification. I found myself listening—to conversations, to radio announcers or television reporters, to dialogue in films—or reading—books, magazines, newspapers, cereal boxes, instruction manuals—for the sole purpose of picking out grammatical lapses, which I would then make the topics of monographs.

To hone your own skills, you may want to try your hand at something similar. Choose as your first topic an aspect of language—grammar or diction—which you find particularly irksome, something that repeatedly sends you to the dictionary or other reference, that leaves you feeling ill at ease or unsure of yourself. Take this hobgoblin, this bothersome bugbear, and slay it. Slay it with humor or wit, or with the sword point of seriousness. Whatever weapon you choose, lay the issue to rest by writing the best piece you can. Then...

Submit it for possible publication. Or show it to your friends. Or keep it for your own amusement. You can even choose to do all three! Tackle enough of these problems, write enough monographs, and you could find yourself an expert on the finer points of usage. If nothing else, you'll impress your editors, and your readers, with your command of the English language.]

Warning: reading the following monograph may induce a headache and cause you to lie down.

When you sleep, you *lie* down. It was last night that you *lay* down (as you have *lain* down many times in the past). Lie, lay, lain: it's as simple as that.

The confusion comes with *lay*. Whereas *to lie* (of which *lay* is the past tense) is intransitive and does not take an object, the verb *to lay* insists on one. Lay down your arms. Lay your head upon my shoulder. Yesterday you laid the tile in your bathroom. My neighbor's hens have laid many eggs over the years.

Compare:

to lie (rest, recline): lie, lay, lain

to lay (place or set down): lay, laid, laid

Before I lay this subject aside (and lie down for a much deserved snooze) let me just add that, like George Washington, I would never *lie* to you. Lie, lied, lied. That's the truth.

Here's to You, Mrs. Malaprop

In Sheridan's play *The Rivals* one of the characters, Mrs. Malaprop, frequently misuses words. "As headstrong as an allegory on the banks of the Nile" is a typical solecism committed by the good lady. A malapropism, therefore, is a humorous misuse of words.

But there is nothing funny about the decay of the English language. When two words having meanings distinct from one another are used interchangeably, as if they both meant the same thing, the language suffers, and we as writers or readers are among the losers.

Two such words are *disinterested* and *uninterested*. They are not synonyms. *Disinterested* means impartial; *uninterested* means indifferent, unconcerned. A disinterested person is one who is unbiased. An uninterested person is one who is bored.

If you are uninterested in such distinctions let me, as a disinterested friend and mentor, advise that you consider taking up a career other than writing.

The Plane Truth

The craft of writing seldom enjoys plane sailing.

Plane sailing? Surely I meant to say *plain* sailing.

Au contraire.

In the days of the great sailing ships, navigators when setting a course on the open seas had to take into account the earth's curvature. If they failed to do so, they risked ending up off course, perhaps a continent or two away from their intended destination.

But when our intrepid sailors, after days, months, or even years of traversing the ocean, finally neared their goal they could ignore the world's rotundity. (Would that I could ignore mine!) Charts used for sailing along coasts, since they represented only a tiny portion of the earth's surface, could project a course on a geometric *plane*.

So when the captain announced, "It's all plane sailing now," he meant that having survived the perils of the high seas he could at last breathe easy and use simple charts as a guide.

If only the craft of good writing sailed so smoothly!

Return to Gender, Sex Unknown

[This next monograph falls into that category of the forlorn known as Lost Causes. Read it, Dear Reader, then—with a tear in your eye—relegate it to Limbo. Like Lyme Disease and other latter-day plagues, the use of gender *to mean* sex *is here to stay.]*

Who said grammarians don't care about sex? Of course we do. We care so much that we become upset when *gender* is substituted for *sex*.

The two words are not interchangeable.

Gender (I won't bother to define *sex*; we all know what that is) is a grammatical term referring to categories, such as feminine, masculine, or neuter, into which in some languages words are divided.

The division often has little or nothing to do with sex. In Spanish for example *lodo*, a word meaning *mud*, is masculine, whereas *comadreja*, the word for weasel, is feminine. I can't speak for others, but I know that neither of these turns me on. A sexy character, however, in the hands of a good writer . . . Or, better yet, a sexy character in *my* hands . . .

Well, you get the point. When a writer, in an otherwise excellent essay on sexual stereotypes in literature, refers to the *gender* of characters, she is in danger of engendering an adverse reaction in her grammatically sensitive readers.

Characters have sex, not gender.

Damned If You Do . . .

[Let this brief essay serve as a warning to the conscientious. No matter how proficient with English you become, much of the time you will simply be casting pearls before swine.]

Some days you just can't win.

You write *Richard the Lion Heart* and your copy editor, no doubt with a supercilious smirk at your presumed carelessness, "corrects" it to Richard the *Lion-Hearted*.

We associate lions with courage and strength, and lion-hearted Richard my have been, but if you consult your history texts you'll find him referred to as Richard *Coeur de Lion*. He earned the epithet, the story goes, by reaching down the throat of a lion and tearing the creature's heart out.

Or you write "toe the line" and it ends up in print as "tow the line." The phrase, which derives from the field of sports, refers to the starting line—a thing you can toe, but certainly not tow.

But be not of faint heart. Matters could be worse. The phrase could end up as "tow the lion," which is better I suppose than having a tiger by its tale.

I Covet Your Skull

"Would you have any objection to my running my finger along your parietal fissure?"

This question is asked of Sherlock Holmes by Dr. James Mortimer in *The Hound of the Baskervilles*. The good country doctor, an accomplished medical scientist, then states: "A cast of your skull, sir, until the original is available, would be an ornament to any anthropological museum. It is not my intention to be fulsome, but I confess that I covet your skull."

Fulsome, as used by Dr. Mortimer, means "excessively insincere." It can also mean "loathsome" or "disgusting." These are its only acceptable meanings. *Fulsome* does not refer to abundance or plenitude. "Our hosts furnished us with a fulsome repast," is an egregious misuse of the word and will not earn the author praise, fulsome or otherwise.

A similarly troublesome word is *noisome*, which means "filthy; disgusting: evil-smelling" or "harmful." *Noisome*, however, has no connection with *noise*, other than sharing the same first four letters. The author of a recent article in *The New Yorker* played on this similarity. Reporting on a law suit that began as a complaint by one tenant against another regarding excessive noise, but which later involved the possible use of hazardous chemicals, he wrote: "If [the upstairs tenant's work] was potentially noisome as well as noisy, the board would have no choice but to stop it."

And that just about *-somes* it up.

A Brief Distillation

If this entry in what I hope is an otherwise sober book turns out to be somewhat incoherent, blame it on the thoroughness of my research. I've only now returned, after many hours of conscientious imbibing, from my liquor cabinet.

Why is it, I wondered, that sometimes you see *whiskey* spelled with an *e*, and sometimes without?

In a blind tasting test (the blindness came toward the end of the tasting), I determined that *whiskey* with an *e* is the spelling for the American distillation, *whisky* lacking an *e* the spelling for the Scotch and Canadian. Here are my notes (copied from the labels on bottles from five random samplings):

imported blended Scots whisky
sour mash: Kentucky straight Bourbon whiskey
Canadian whisky
American whiskey
blended Scotch whisky

Further research shows that the spelling for the Irish version of the beverage is the same as for the American: with an *e*.

The word—*whiskey* or *whisky*—derives from the Gaelic *usquebaugh*, meaning "water of life." If you wonder how that came about—how did a word beginning with a *u* and ending with an *h* become a word beginning with a *w* and ending with a *y*?—try saying *usquebaugh* after five shots of the stuff and—if you can still maneuver your tongue—you'll more than likely come out with something at least approximating *whiskey*.

If you paid careful attention, you saw from my notes that I sampled both a *Scots* and a *Scotch* whisky. Is there a difference? For a brief monograph on the subject please refer to the next entry.

Scotch That Notion!

Writers who habitually misuse words will not, in the end, escape scot-free. They will pay the ultimate price: rejection.

The *scot*—a word meaning "payment"—of *scot-free* has a complex etymology (Middle English, Old French, Old Norse, and one or two other sources) but bears no relation to the proper name *Scot* (a native of Scotland).

I hope you will agree that this book is chock-full of such useful information.

The *chock* of *chock-full* refers to a block or wedge placed under something, such as a wheel, to keep it from moving. Another word for such a device is *scotch*. This *scotch* bears no relation to the *Scotch* (a name, considered by some to be offensive, for the people of Scotland). Nor does an entirely different word, the verb *scotch*, have anything to do with Scotland, despite the fact that its most famous use in literature was by the Scotsman Macbeth: "We have scotched the snake, not killed it."

Scotch as used by Macbeth means "to wound without killing, so as to render harmless." *Scotch* does not mean—as it is frequently misused—"to kill outright, absolutely and completely." Purists will insist on restricting the word to the original meaning of "to cripple" and will not allow it to mean "to kill." Let us, however, not enter this fray. It is a lost cause. In other words, scotch the notion.

❖

All of the preceding is by way of a preamble to the real subject of this monograph: the various uses, and misuses, of *Scots*, *Scotch*, and *Scottish* as applied to the people and things of Scotland.

In these days of political correctness we should take care not to offend *Scots* by referring to them as the *Scotch*. A Scotsman (or Scotswoman) does not like to be called a Scotchman (or Scotchwoman). The dialect of Scotland is *Scots*, not *Scottish*, though the English often refer to it as *Scotch*.

Scotch as an adjective is frequently frowned upon in Scotland. However, Scotch whisky is perfectly proper, as are Scotch tweed and Scotch broth. It's okay to have Scotch eggs for breakfast or tea. A Scotch terrier, on the other hand, is more properly a *Scottish* terrier.

Scottish—as in "the Scottish Highlands"—is generally the adjective of preference for things pertaining to Scotland and things native to it.

If like me you are thoroughly confused by all of this, pour yourself a shot of Scotch and treat yourself to a Scotch woodcock for lunch or, just to be different, a Welsh (not *Welch*) rabbit (not *rarebit*).

Who Gives a Whom?

In the phrase "to whom it may concern" *whom* is the object of the preposition *to*, right?

Wrong.

Whom is the object of the verb *concern*. The object of the preposition *to* is the entire clause, *whom it may concern*.

This message is intended for whoever has trouble with *who* and *whom*. Note that I did not write *whomever*. That's because *whoever* is the subject of the clause "whoever has trouble," and not the object of the proposition *for*.

Many writers feel that *whom* is pedantic. Certainly in everyday speech *who* is often used when *whom* would be grammatically correct. Who did you give the money to? Who did you see at the theater? This usage is widely accepted.

What is not accepted is the opposite: using *whom* when *who* is required. "John, having learned *whom* the visitor was, regretted his rudeness." In that sentence *whom* should be *who*, since it is not the object of *learned* (the entire clause is) but rather a predicate pronoun (*the visitor was who*).

If we don't give a hoot about *who* and *whom*, we may become writers whom others (such as careful editors) do not heed.

Opposites Attract?

An oddity of the English language is that it contains words that mean the opposite of themselves.

For instance, consider humble *let*. *Let* commonly means to allow. But it also has the somewhat archaic meaning of obstruct or hinder—still used in its noun form in the legal phrase, "without let or hindrance."

Cleave is another such word. It can mean to split or separate, or it can mean the opposite: to adhere, cling or stick fast. (*Fast* itself means moving quickly, or the opposite, fixed firmly in place.)

Cleave in the first sense comes from the Old English word *cleofan*. The past tense is *cleft* or *cleaved* or *clove*, the past participle *cleft*, *cleaved* or *cloven*. If that's not enough to convince you to convert to an easier language, such as Chinese, consider the other meaning of *cleave*, which descends from the Old English word *cleofian*. Its past tense is *cleaved* or *clove* (or even *clave*) but never *cleft*. Let's not even venture to consider the past participle.

If you can ravel the sense from all this, you won't become raveled in a tangle of words. *Ravel*: 1. to clarify by separating the aspects of; 2. to become tangled or confused.

Ravel, in other words, means to *unravel*. Is it any wonder the devil has a *cloven* (or should that be *cleft*) hoof?

Well, I'll Be Hanged!

Don't you be hanged for the crime of using the wrong verb form.

Objects are *hung*. People are *hanged*.

"Joe hung the clothes outside on the line to dry. Mary has already hung the painting on the wall."

Hang, hung, hung.

"They hanged the murderer at dawn. I may as well be hanged for a sheep as for a goat."

Hang, hanged, hanged (in the sense of capital punishment).

It's as simple as that. Nothing to get hung up about.

What's for Dessert?

The poet Andrew Marvell reminded his coy mistress that, "Yonder all before us lie / deserts of vast eternity."

Deserts are barren, desolate places. On the other hand, *desserts* are the last course of a meal, sweet foods such as fruit or pie or cake or ice cream. The two words are spelled and pronounced differently.

Children are sometimes punished for misbehavior at the dinner table by not being allowed to eat *dessert*. A person who acts wrongly and is then punished is said to receive his or her just *deserts*. Not his or her just *desserts*. The two words, though spelled differently, are pronounced the same. But the former means "that which is deserved or merited."

The finest dessert that a writer can enjoy is the sweet taste of success. Writers who are careless with words, however, get their just deserts by not getting published.

Before we *desert* (abandon) this subject, let us add a bit more icing to the cake by considering Mount *Desert*, an island in Down East Maine. The preferred pronunciation (at least by those native to the area) is as if the word were spelt *dessert* (that is to say, *desert* when it means *abandon*).

Afterword

So there you have it: everything you'll ever need to know in order to become a successful writer. Well, perhaps not everything; there may be a few things I've left out—enough, no doubt, to fill a dozen average-size encyclopedias.

But on that proverbial journey of a thousand miles, which begins with just one step, you're off to a tottering start, and that's what counts. You are armed with fortitude and forbearance; you are aware of pitfalls to avoid, and you know of guideposts along the way that will help you from getting lost. What more could you ask?

What's that? You want the secrets of how to go about getting your work published?

That, I'm afraid, is the subject for another book. Not one, incidentally, which I have any intention of writing. But I will share with you one little secret: getting published can be more difficult, and time-consuming, and frustrating, than writing an epic poem or a one-thousand page novel, or any number of volumes of short stories.

Can be more difficult, but doesn't have to be. These days, it's easy and relatively inexpensive to self-publish. But is it wise to do so? The answer to that question is one which you'll have to answer for yourself. But if you truly believe in the worth of your work, and decide to self-publish, be prepared to venture out into the world and do battle with the forces of inertia.

Then again, who knows? You may be invited to give readings and talks at libraries—which, you will remember, is how the idea for this book came about.